Open Letter to Comrade Lenin by Herman Gorter
First Prism Key Press Edition 2011

Prism Key Press
New York, NY 10001
PrismKeyPress.com

ISBN-13: 978-1467903240

Open Letter to Comrade Lenin

Herman Gorter

CONTENTS

I wish to draw your attention, Comrade Lenin, and that of the reader, to the fact that this letter was written at the time of the triumphant march of the Russians to Warsaw.

I likewise request you, and the reader, to excuse the frequent repetitions. They were unavoidable, owing to the fact that the tactics of the "Lefts" are still unknown to the workers of most countries.

Herman Gorter.

Introduction

Dear Comrade Lenin,

I have read your brochure on the Radicalism in the Communist movement. It has taught me a great deal, as all your writings have done. For this I feel grateful to you, and doubtless many other comrades feel as I do. Many a trace, and many a germ of this infantile disease, to which without a doubt, I also am a victim, has been chased away by your brochure, or will yet be eradicated by it. Your observations about the confusion that revolution has caused in many brains, is quite right too. I know that. The revolution came so suddenly, and in a way so utterly different from what we expected. Your words will be an incentive to me, once again, and to an even greater extent than before, to base my judgment in all matters of tactics, also in the revolution, exclusively on reality, on the actual class-relations, as they manifest themselves politically and economically.

After having read your brochure I thought all this is right.

But after having considered for a long time whether I would cease to uphold this "Left Wing," and to write articles for the KAPD and the Opposition party in England, I had to decline.

Basis Mistaken.

This seems contradictory. It is due, though, to the fact that the starting-point in the brochure is not right. To my idea you are mistaken in your judgment regarding the analogy of the West-European revolution with the Russian one, regarding the conditions of the West-European revolution, that is to say the class-relations, and this leads you to mistake the cause, from which this Left Wing, the opposition, originates.

Therefore the brochure SEEMS to be right, as long as your starting-point is assumed. If, however (as it should be), your starting point is rejected, the entire brochure is wrong. As all your mistaken, and partly mistaken, judgments converge in your condemnation of the Left movement, especially in Germany and England, and as I firmly intend to defend those of the Left Wing, although, as the leaders know, I do not agree with them on all points, I imagine I had best answer your brochure by a defence of the Left Wing. This will enable me not only to point out its origin (the cause from which it springs), and to prove its right, and merits, in the present stage, and here, in Western Europe, but also, which is of equal importance, to combat the mistaken conceptions that are prevalent in Russia with regard to the West-European Revolution.

Both these points are of importance, as it is on the conception of the West-European revolution that the West-European as well as the Russian tactics depend. I should have hiked to do this at the Moscow Congress, which, however, I was not able to attend.

Two Arguments Refuted.

In the first place I must refute two of your arguments, that may mislead the judgment of comrades or readers. You scoff and sneer at the ridiculous and childish nonsense of the struggle in Germany, at the "dictatorship of the leaders or of the masses," at "from above or below," etc. We quite agree with you, that these should be no questions at all. But we do not agree with your scoffing. For that is the pity of it: in Western-Europe they still are questions. In Western Europe we still have, in many countries, leaders of the type of the Second International; here we are still seeking the right leaders, those that **do not try to dominate the masses**, that do not betray them; and as long as we do not find these leaders, we want to do all things from below, and through the dictatorship of the masses themselves. If I have a mountain-guide, and he should lead me into the abyss, I prefer to do without him. As soon as we have found the right guides, we will stop this searching. Then mass and leader will be really one. This, and nothing else, is what the German and English Left Wing, what we ourselves, mean by these words.

And the same holds good for your second remark, that the leader should form one united whole with class and mass. We quite agree with you. But the question is to find and rear leaders that are really one with the masses. This can only be accomplished by the masses, the political parties and the Trade Unions, by means of the most severe struggle, also inwardly. And the same holds good for iron discipline, and strong centralisation. We want them all right, but not until we have the right leaders. This severest of all struggles, which is now being fought most strenuously in Germany and England, the two countries where Communism is nearest to its realisation, can only be harmed by your scoffing. Your attitude panders to the opportunist elements in the Third International. By this scoffing, you abet the opportunist elements in the Third International.

For it is one of the means by which elements in the Spartakus League and in the BSP, and also in the Communist Parties in many other countries, imposes upon the workers, when they say that the entire question of masses and leader is absurd, is "nonsense and childishness." Through this phrase they avoid, and wish to avoid, all criticism of themselves, the leaders. It is by means of this phrase of an iron discipline and centralisation, that they crush the opposition. And this opportunism is abetted by you.

You should not do this, Comrade. We are only in the introductory stage yet, here in Western Europe. And in that stage it is better to encourage the fighters than the rulers.

I only touch on this quite perfunctorily here. In the course of this writing I will deal with this matter more at length. There is a deeper reason yet why I cannot agree with your brochure. It is the following

11

Difference Between Russia and W. Europe.

On reading your pamphlets, brochures and books, nearly all of which writings filled us with admiration and approbation, we Marxists of Western Europe invariably came to a point where we suddenly grew wary, and on the look-out for a more detailed explanation; and if we failed to find this explanation, we accepted the statement but grudgingly, with all due reservations. This was your statement regarding the workers and the poor peasants. It occurs often, very often. And you always mention both these categories as revolutionary factors all the world over. And nowhere, at least as far as I have read, is there a clear and outspoken recognition of the immense difference which prevails in the matter between Russia (and a few other countries in Eastern Europe) and Western Europe (that is to say Germany, France, England, Belgium, Holland, Switzerland, and the Scandinavian countries, and perhaps even Italy). And yet, in my opinion, the fundamental difference between your conception of the tactics concerning Trade Unionism and Parliamentarism, and that of the so-called Left Wing in Western Europe, lies mainly in this point.

Of course you know this difference as well as I do, only you failed to draw from it the conclusions for the tactics in Western Europe, at least as far as I am able to judge from your works. These conclusions you have not taken into consideration, and consequently your judgement on these West-European tactics is false.

And this is all the more dangerous, because this phrase of yours is parroted automatically in all the Communist Parties of Western Europe, even by Marxists. To judge from all Communist papers, magazines and brochures, and from all public assemblies, one might even surmise that a revolt of the poor peasants in Western Europe might break out at any moment! Nowhere is the great difference with Russia pointed out, and thus the judgment, also of the proletariat, is led astray. Because in Russia you were able to triumph with the help of a large class of poor peasants, you represent things in such a way, as if we in Western Europe are also going to have that help. Because you, in Russia, have triumphed exclusively through this help, you wish to make us believe that here also we will triumph through this help. You do this by means of your silence with regard to this question, as it stands in Western Europe, and your entire tactics are based on this representation.

Poor Peasants Decisive Factor.

This representation, however, is not the truth. There is an enormous difference between Russia and Western Europe. In general the importance of the poor peasants as a revolutionary factor decreases from east to west. In some Parts of Asia, China, and India, in the event of a revolution, this class would be the absolutely decisive factor; in Russia it constitutes an indispensable and, indeed, one of the main factors; in Poland, and in a few states of South-Eastern and Central Europe, it is still of importance for the revolution, but further West its attitude grows ever more antagonistic towards the revolution.

Russia had an industrial proletariat of some seven or eight millions. The number of poor peasants, however, amounted to about 25 millions. (I beg you to excuse the inevitable numerical errors; I have to quote from memory, as this letter should be despatched with all speed). When Kerensky failed to give these poor peasants the soil, you knew that before long they would come to you, the minute they should become aware of the fact. This is not so in Western Europe, and will not become so either; in the countries of Western Europe, which I have named, conditions of that sort do not exist.

The poor peasant here hives under conditions quite different from those of Russia. Though often terrible, they are not as appalling as they were there. As farmers or owners, the poor peasants possess a piece of land. The excellent means of transport enables them often to sell their goods. At the very worst they can mostly provide their own food. During the last ten years things have improved somewhat for them. Now, during and since the war, they can obtain high prices. They are indispensable, the import of foodstuffs being very limited. Regularly, therefore, they will be able to get high prices. They are supported by Capitalism. Capitalism will maintain them, as long as it can maintain itself. In your country, the position of the poor peasants was far more terrible. With you, therefore, the poor peasants had a political, revolutionary programme, and were organised in a political, revolutionary party: with the social-revolutionaries. With us this is nowhere the case. Moreover, in Russia there was an enormous amount of landed property to be divided, large estates, crown lands, government land, and the estates held by the monasteries. But the Communists of Western Europe, what can they offer to the poor peasants, to win them to their side?

Nothing to Offer Peasants.

Germany counted, before the war, from four to five million poor peasants (up to two hectares). Only eight or nine millions, however, were employed in actual large-scale industries (over 100 hectares). If the Communists were to divide all of these, the poor peasants would still be poor peasants, as the seven or eight million field-labourers also claim their share. And they cannot even divide them, as they will use them as large-scale industries.

These numbers show that in Western Europe there are comparatively few poor peasants; that, therefore, the auxiliary forces, if there were any at all, would be very few in numbers.

The Communists in Germany, therefore, except in relatively insignificant regions, do not even have the means to win over the poor peasants. For the medium and small industries will surely not be expropriated. And it is practically the same in the case of the four or five million poor peasants in France, and also for Switzerland, Belgium, Holland, and two of the Scandinavian countries. Everywhere small and medium sized industry prevails. Arid even in Italy there is no absolute certainty; not to mention England, which counts only some one or two hundred thousand peasants.

Neither will they be attracted by the promise that under Communism they will be exempt from rent-paying and mortgage-rent. For with Communism they see the approach of civil war, the loss of markets, and general destruction.

Unless, therefore, there should come a crisis far more terrible than the present one in Germany, a crisis, indeed, far exceeding the horrors of any other crises that ever were before, the poor peasants in Western Europe will side with Capitalism, as long as it has any life left.

Industrial Workers Stand Alone.

The workers in Western Europe stand all alone. Only a very slight portion of the lower middle class will help them. And these are economically insignificant. The workers will have to make the revolution all by themselves. Here is the great difference as compared to Russia.

Possibly you will say, Comrade Lenin, that this was the case in Russia. There also the proletariat has made the revolution all by itself. It is only after the revolution that the poor peasants joined. You are right, and yet the difference is immense.

You knew with absolute certainty that the peasants would dome to you, and that they would dome quickly. You knew that Kerensky would not, and could not give them the land. You knew that they would not help Kerensky long. You had a magic charm, "The Land to the Peasants," by means of which you would win them in the course of a few months to the side of the proletariat. We, on the other hand, are certain that for some time to dome the poor peasants, all over Western Europe, will side with Capitalism.

You will possibly say that, although in Germany there is

15

no great mass of poor peasants whose assistance can be relied on, the millions of proletarians that side as yet with the bourgeoisie are sure to come round. That, therefore, the place of the poor peasants in Russia will here be taken by the proletarians, so that there is help all the same. This representation is also fundamentally wrong, and the immense difference remains.

The Russian peasants joined the proletariat AFTER Capitalism has been defeated; but when the German workers that are now as yet on the side of Capitalism join the ranks of the Communists, the struggle against Capitalism will begin in real earnest.

The revolution in Russia was terrible for the proletariat in the long years of its development and it is terrible now, after the victory. But at the actual time of revolution it was easy, and this was due to the peasants.

With us it is quite the contrary. In its development the revolution was easy, and it will be easy afterwards; but its actual coming will be terrible – more terrible, perhaps, than any other revolution ever was, for Capitalism, which in your country was weak and only slightly rooted as it were to feudalism, the middle ages and even barbarism, here in our country is strong and widely organised and deeply rooted, and the lower middle classes as well as the peasants, who always side with the strongest, with the exception of a shallow and economically unimportant layer, will stand with Capitalism until the very end.

The revolution in Russia was victorious with the help of the poor peasants. This should always be borne in mind here in Western Europe and all the world over. But the workers in Western Europe stand alone: this should never be forgotten in Russia.

The proletariat in Western Europe stands alone.

This is the absolute truth: and on this truth our tactics

must be based. All tactics that are not based on this are false, and lead the proletariat to terrible defeat.

Practice also has proved that these assertions are true, for the poor peasants in Western Europe have not only no programme and failed to claim the land, but they do not even stir now that Communism is approaching. As I have observed before, this statement is not to be taken absolutely literally. There are regions in Western Europe where, as we have mentioned before, landed property on a large scale is predominant, and where the peasants are therefore in favour of Communism. There are yet other regions where the local conditions are such that the poor peasants may be won for Communism. But these regions are comparatively small. Neither do I wish to imply that quite at the dose of the revolution, when all things are coming down, there will be no poor peasants doming to our side. They undoubtedly will. That is why we must carry on an unceasing propaganda amongst them. Our tactics, however, must be adopted for the beginning and for the course of the revolution. What I mean is the general trend, the general tendency of conditions. And it is on these alone that our tactics must be based.

From this there follows in the first place – and it should be clearly, emphatically and plainly stated – that in Western Europe the real revolution, that is to say the overthrow of Capitalism, and the erection and permanent institution of Communism, for the time being is possible only in those countries where the proletariat BY ITSELF is strong enough against all the other classes – in Germany, England, and Italy, where the help of the poor peasants is not possible. In the other countries the revolution can only be prepared as yet by means of propaganda, organisation and fighting. The revolution itself can only follow when the economic conditions will be thus much shaken through the revolution in the big States (Russia, Germany, and England), that the bourgeois class will have grown sufficiently weak. For you will agree with me that we cannot base our tactics on events that may dome, but that may

17

also never happen (help from the Russian armies, risings in India, terrible crises, etc., etc.).

That you should have failed to recognise this truth concerning the importance of the poor peasants, Comrade, is your first great mistake, and likewise that of the Executive in Moscow and of the International Congress.

What does it mean with regard to tactics, this fact that the proletariat of Western Europe stands all alone: that it has no prospect of any help whatsoever from any other class?

It means, in the first place, that the demands made on the masses are far greater here than in Russia – that, therefore, the proletarian mass is of far greater importance in the revolution. And in the second place that the importance of the leaders is proportionately smaller.

For the Russian masses, the proletarians, knew for certain, and already saw during the war, and in part before their very eyes, that the peasants would soon be on their side. The German proletarians, to take them first, know that they will be opposed by German Capitalism in its entirety, with all its classes.

It is true that already before the war the German proletarians numbered from nineteen to twenty million actual workers, of a population of seventy million, but they stood alone against all the other classes. They are opposed by a Capitalism that is immeasurably stronger than that of Russia – and they are UNARMED. The Russians were armed.

From every German proletarian therefore, from every individual, the revolution demands a far greater courage and spirit of sacrifice than was necessary in Russia.

This is the outcome of the economic class relations in Germany, and not of some theory or idea risen from the brain of revolutionary romantics or intellectuals!

Unless the entire class or at least the great majority stand up for the revolution personally, with almost superhuman force, in opposition to all the other classes, the revolution will fail; for you will agree with me again that on determining our tactics we should reckon with our own forces, not with those from outside – on Russian help, for instance.

The proletariat almost unarmed, alone, without help, against a closely united Capitalism, means for Germany that every proletarian must be a conscious fighter, every proletarian a hero; and it is the same for all Western Europe.

For the majority of the proletariat to turn into conscious, steadfast fighters, into real Communists, they must be greater, immeasurably greater, here than in Russia, in an absolute as well as a relative sense. And once more: this is the outcome, not of the representations, the dreams of some intellectual, or poet, but of the purest realities.

And as the importance of the class grows, the importance of the leaders becomes relatively less. This does not mean that we must not have the very best of leaders. The best are not good enough; we are trying hard to find them. It only means that the importance of the leaders, as compared to that of the masses, is decreasing.

For you, who had to win a country of 160 million, with the help of seven or eight million, the importance of the leaders was certainly immense! To triumph over so many, with so few, is in the first place a matter of tactics. To do as you did, Comrade, to win such a huge land, with such small forces, but with assistance from outside, all depends in the first place on the tactics of the leader. When you, Comrade Lenin, started the struggle with a small gathering of proletarians, it was in the first place your tactics that in the crucial moments waged the battles and won the poor peasants.

But what about Germany? There the cleverest of tactics, the greatest clarity, even the genius of leaders, cannot attain much. There you have an inexorable class enmity, one against all the others. There the proletarian class must tip the scales for itself – through its power, its numbers. Its power, however, is based above all on its quality, the enemy being so mighty and so endlessly better organised and armed than the proletariat.

You opposed the Russian possessing classes, as David opposed Goliath. David was little, but he had a deadly weapon. The German, the English, the West-European proletariat oppose Capitalism as one giant does another. Between them all depends on strength – strength of body, and above all of mind.

Have you not observed, Comrade Lenin, that in Germany there are no great leaders? They are all quite ordinary men. This points to the fact that this revolution must in the first place be the work of the masses, not of the leaders.

To my idea this is something more wonderful and grand than has ever been, and it is an indication of what Communism will be.

And as it is in Germany, it is in all Western Europe, for everywhere the proletariat stands alone.

The revolution of the masses, of the workers – of the masses of workers alone, for the first time in the world.

And not because thus it is good, or beautiful, or conceived in someone's brain, but because the economic and class relations will it.

In other words, and to read the matter as clearly as possible: the relation between the West-European and the Russian revolution can be demonstrated by means of the following comparison:

Supposing that in an Asiatic country like China or British India, where only one half a per cent of the inhabitants are industrial proletarians, and 80 per cent small peasants, a revolution should break out, and should be successfully carried through by those small peasants under the lead of the politically and socially more trained proletarians that were united in local

20

trade unions and co-operatives. If these Chinese or Indian workers proclaimed to them:

"We have won through our local trade unions and co-operatives, and now you must do the same with regard to your revolution," what would the Russian workers have replied? They would have said:

"Dear friends, this is impossible. Our country is far more developed than yours. With us not half, but three per cent of the population are industrial proletarians. Our Capitalism is more powerful than yours, therefore we need better and more powerful organisations than you did."

From this difference between Russia and Western Europe there follows likewise:

1. That when you, or the Executive in Moscow, or the opportunist Communists of Western Europe, of the Spartakus League, or of the English Communist Party, say: "It is nonsense to fight about the question of leader or masses," that you in that case are wrong as regards us, not only because we are yet trying to find those leaders, but also because for you this question has quite another meaning.

2. That when you say to us: "Leader and mass must be one inseparable whole," you are wrong, not only because we are striving for that unity, but also because that question has another meaning for you than for us.

3. That when you may: "In the Communist Party there should reign iron discipline, and absolute military centralisation," this is wrong, not only because we are seeking iron discipline and strong centralisation, but also because this question has a different meaning for us and for you.

4. That when you say: "We acted in such and such a way in Russia (after the Kornilov offensive for instance, or some other episode), or entered Parliament during this or that period, or we remained in the trade unions, and therefore the German proletariat must do the same," all this means absolutely nothing,

21

and need not or cannot be applicable in any way. For the West-European class relations in the struggle, in the revolution, are quite different from those of Russia.

5. That when you wish to force upon us tactics that were good in Russia – tactics, for instance, that were based, consciously or unconsciously, on the conviction that here the poor peasants will soon join the proletariat – in other words, that the proletariat does not stand alone – that your tactics, which you prescribe, and which are followed here, will lead the West-European proletariat into ruin, and the most terrible defeat.

6. That when you, or the Executive in Moscow, or the opportunist elements in Western Europe, like the Central Board of the Spartakus League or the BSP, try to compel us to follow opportunist tactics (opportunism always seeks the support of outside elements, that forsake the proletariat), you are wrong.

The general bases on which the tactics in Western Europe must be founded are these: the recognition that the proletariat stands alone, that it is to expect no help, that the importance of the mass is greater, and that of the leaders relatively smaller.

This was not seen by Radek when he was in Germany, not by the Executive in Moscow, nor by you, as is evident from your words.

And it is on these bases that the tactics of the Kommunistische-Arbeiter Partei in Germany, the Communist Party of Sylvia Pankhurst, and the majority of the Amsterdam Commission, as appointed by Moscow, are founded.

It is on these grounds that they strive, above all, to raise the masses as a whole, and the individuals to a higher level, to educate them one by one to be revolutionary fighters, by making them realise (not through theory only, but especially by practice), that all depends on them, that they are to expect nothing from foreign help, very little from leaders, and all from themselves.

Theoretically, therefore, and apart from private utterances, minor questions and excrescences, which like those of Wolffheim and Laufenberg, are inevitable in the first phases of a movement, the view taken by these parties and comrades is quite right, and your opposition absolutely wrong.

On going from the East to the West of Europe, we traverse at a given moment an economic boundary. It runs from the Baltic to the Mediterranean, somewhere from Danzig to Venice. This line divides two worlds. West of this line there is a practically absolute domination of industrial, commercial and financial capital, united in the most highly developed banking capital.

Even agricultural capital is subject to, or has been compelled to unite with, this capital. This capital is organised to the utmost degree, and converges in the most firmly established State Governments of the world.

East of the line there is neither this gigantic development of industrial, commercial, transport and banking capital, not its almost absolute domination, nor, consequently, the firmly established modern State.

It would be marvellous, indeed, if the tactics of the revolutionary proletariat west of this boundary-line were the same as in the east!

1. In *State and Revolution*, for instance, you write (page 67): "The greatest majority of the peasantry in every capitalist country that has any peasantry at all, is oppressed by the government, and so thirsting for the latter's overthrow, for 'cheap' government. The proletariat is called upon to carry this into execution ..." The trouble is, however, that the peasantry does not thirst for Communism.

2. The Agrarian Theses of Moscow acknowledges this.

3. I have no statistical data for Sweden and Spain.

4. In the brochure, The World Revolution, I have emphatically

pointed out this difference between Russia and Western Europe. The development of the German Revolution has proved that any judgment was even too optimistic. In Italy it is possible that the poor peasants will side with the proletariat.

5. You, Comrade, will surely not try and win in an argument by taking the assertions of your opponent in too absolute a sense, as small minds do. My above remark, therefore, is meant for the latter.

6. Of course I had to take the pre-war figures, and have made the increase in proletarians after the last census (of 1909) proportionate to that before.

7. I do not touch here on the fact that through this other relation of numbers (20 million to 70 million in Germany!) the importance of the mass and the leaders, and the relation between mass, party and leaders, also in the course and at the close of the revolution here, will differ from those of Russia.

8. So far, at least.

9. It has struck me that in this controversy you almost invariably make use of private, and not public voices of the opposition.

The Question of the Trade Unions

Having brought forward the general theoretical bases, I will now proceed to prove, also by practice, that the Left Wing in Germany and England is right in general principles – on the questions of the Trade Unions and of parliamentarism.

First we will take the question of the Trade Unions.

As parliamentarism embodies the spiritual, thus the Trade Union movement embodies the material power of the leaders over the masses of the workers. Under capitalism the Trade Unions constitute the natural organisations for uniting the proletariat, and as such Marx, already from the very beginning, has demonstrated their importance. Under a more developed capitalism, and to a greater extent even in the age of imperialism, the Trade Unions have ever more become gigantic unions, with a trend of development, equal to that of the bourgeois State bodies themselves. They have produced a class of officials, a bureaucracy, that controls all the engines of power of the organisation, the finances, the press, the appointment of lower officials; often it is invested with even greater power, so that from a servant of the rank and file, it has become the master, identifying itself with the organisation. The Trade Unions can be compared to the State and its bureaucracy, also in this: that, notwithstanding the democracy that is supposed to reign there, the members are unable to enforce their will against the bureaucracy; every revolt is broken against the cleverly constructed apparatus of official ordinances and statutes, before it has been able even to shake the highest regions.

Only the most tenacious perseverance over several years can obtain even a moderate result, which mostly remains restricted to a change of persons. In the last few years, before and after the war, in England, Germany, and America, this often gave rise to rebellions of the members, who started strikes on their own account, against the will of the leaders, or the decrees of the union itself. That this should seem natural, and be accepted as such, is an indication in itself that the organisation does not represent the totality of the members, but something altogether foreign to them; and the workers do not control their union, but that the union is placed over them as an outside power against which they can rebel – a power which, all the same, has its origin in themselves: again, therefore, an analogy with the State. Once the revolt is over, the old domination begins again. In spite of the hatred and impotent exasperation of the masses, this domination manages to maintain itself, owing to the indifference and lack of clear insight, and of a united, indomitable will in the masses, and upheld as it is by the inner need for the Trade Unions, the only means the workers have to gain strength through unity, in their struggle against capital.

Warning of TU Influence

Fighting against capital, in a constant opposition against its tendency of increasing misery, and enabling the working class, through the restriction of these tendencies, to keep the existence the Trade Union movement, has played its part under capitalism, and has thus become itself a member of capitalist society. It is only at the beginning of the revolution, when the proletariat, from a member of capitalist society, is turned into the annihilator of this society, that the Trade Union finds itself in opposition to the proletariat.

That which Marx and Lenin demonstrated for the State: that its organisation, in spite of formal democracy, makes it impossible to turn it into an Instrument of the proletarian revolution, must also hold good therefore for the Trade Union organisations. Their counter-revolutionary power cannot be destroyed or weakened through a change of staff, through the replacing of reactionary leaders by radical or revolutionary elements.

It is the form of organisation that renders the masses as good as powerless, and prevents them from turning the Trade Unions into the organs of their will. The revolution can triumph only if it completely destroys this organisation: that is to say, if it alters the form of organisation so fundamentally as to turn it into something altogether different. The Soviet system, the construction from within, is not only able to uproot and abolish the State, but also the Trade Union bureaucracy: it will constitute not only the new political organs of the proletariat as opposed to capitalism, but likewise the foundation for the new Trade Unions. In the party factions in Germany, the idea of a form of organisation being revolutionary has been mocked at, because it is only the revolutionary sentiment, the revolutionary mind of the members, that matters. However, if the most important part of the revolution consists in the masses conducting their own concerns – the control of society and production – then every form of organisation that does not allow the masses to rule and to guide for themselves, must needs be counter-revolutionary and harmful, and as such it must be replaced by another form, which is revolutionary in so far as it allows the workers to decide matters for themselves.

Through their very nature the Trade Unions are useless arms for the West-European revolution! Apart from the fact that they have become tools of capitalism, and that they are in the hands of traitors, apart from the fact that through their nature they are bound to make slaves of the members, no matter what the leaders may be, they are also unfit for use generally.

The Harder Task of Europe.

The Trade Unions are too weak in the contest against the most highly-organised capital in Western-European States. These latter are powerful: the unions are not. To a great extent the Trade Unions are Professional Unions as yet, which cannot make a revolution, if it were for that fact alone. And in so far as they are industrial unions, they are not founded on the factories, on the workshops themselves, and are consequently weak. Also they are more unions for mutual aid than for struggle, dating as they do from the days of the small bourgeoisie. Even before the revolution, their organisation was already inadequate for the struggle; for the Revolution itself it cannot serve at all – in Western Europe. For the factories, the workers in the factories, make the revolution, not in the industries and professions, but in the workshops. Moreover, these unions are far too slow-working, complicated instruments, good only for the evolutionary period. Even if the revolution should not succeed right away, and we had once more to revert to peaceful action for a while, the Trade Unions would have to be destroyed and replaced by industrial unions, on a basis of industrial or workshop organisation. And with these miserable Trade Unions, that must be done away with in any case, they want to make the revolution! The workers in Western Europe need WEAPONS for the revolution. The only weapons for the revolution in Western Europe are *Industrial Organisations*. And these united into ONE big whole!

The workers in Western Europe need the very best weapons. They stand alone: they have no help. And therefore they need these industrial organisations. In Germany and England they need them at once, because there the revolution is nearest at hand. The other countries must have them as soon as possible, as soon as we can build them.

It is no good at all, Comrade Lenin, your saying: in Russia we did it in such and such a way, for in the first place you had no organisations that were so inadequate for the struggle as many of the Trade Unions are here. You had industrial unions. Secondly, your workers were more revolutionary in spirit. Thirdly, the organisation of the capitalists was weak: and the State also. And in the fourth place, and this is the main point: you had help. You did not need the very best of weapons. We stand alone, we must have them. We will not win unless we have them. We will be defeated over and over again, unless we have them.

28

Other grounds than material ones also demonstrate this.

Recall in your mind, Comrade, how things were in Germany, before and during the war. The Trade Unions, the far too weak but only means, were entirely in the hands of the leaders, who used them as dead machines on behalf of capitalism. Then the revolution broke out. The Trade Unions were used by the leaders and the masses of members as a weapon against the revolution. It was through their help, through their cooperation, through their leaders, nay, partly even through their members that the revolution was murdered. The Communists saw their own brothers being shot with the cooperation of the Trade Unions. Strikes in favour of the revolution were prevented, rendered impossible. Do you hold it possible, Comrade, that under such conditions revolutionary workers should remain in these unions? Especially when these latter are utterly inadequate instruments for the revolution! In my opinion this is a physical impossibility. What would you yourself have done, as a member of a political party, that of the Menshevists for instance, if these had acted thus in the revolution? You would have split the Party (if you had not already done so)! You will reply:

this was a political party, it is different in the case of a Trade Union. I believe you are mistaken. In the revolution, during the revolution, every Trade Union, every workers' union even, is a political party – either pro- or counterrevolutionary.

In your article, however, you say, and you will do so now: these emotional impulses must be conquered, for the sake of unity and Communist propaganda. I will show you, by means of concrete examples, that during the revolution this was impossible in Germany. For these questions must also be considered quite concretely. Let us suppose that Germany had 100,000 really revolutionary dock labourers, 100,000 revolutionary metal workers, and 100,000 revolutionary miners; that these were willing to strike, to fight, to die for the revolution, and that the other millions were not. What are these

300,000 to do? They must in the first place unite, and form a fighting league. This you acknowledge. Without organisation workers can do nothing. Now a new league against old unions, even if the workers remain in the old ones, is a split already; if not formally, at any rate actually, in reality. Next, however, the members of the new league need a press, meetings, localities, a salaried staff. This requires heaps of money. And the German workers possess next to nothing. In order to keep the new league going, they must needs, whether they like it or not, leave the old one. Thus we see that, concretely considered, that which you, Comrade, propose, is impossible.

Build on New Foundations.

However, there are better material grounds yet. The German workers who left the Trade Unions, that wished to destroy them, that created the industrial organisations and workers' unions, stood IN THE REVOLUTION. It was necessary to fight at ONCE. The revolution was there. The Trade Unions refused to fight. What is the good then of saying: remain in the Trade Unions, propagate your ideas, you will grow stronger, and become the majority. Apart from the fact that the minority would be strangled, as is the custom there, this would be quite fine, and also the Left Wing would try it, if there were only time to do so. But it was impossible to wait. The revolution had begun. And it is still going on!

IN THE REVOLUTION (mind, Comrade, it was in the revolution that the German workers split the Party, and created their Workers' Union) the revolutionary workers will always separate themselves from the social-patriots. In the struggle, no other way is possible. No matter what you, and the Moscow Executive, and the International Congress say, and no matter how much you dislike a split in the Party, it will always take place, on psychological and material grounds, because the workers cannot in the long run tolerate the Trade Unions shooting them, and because there has to be fighting.

That is why the Left Wing has created the Workers' Unions; and as they believe that the revolution in Germany is not over yet, but it will proceed to the final victory, they keep them up.

Comrade Lenin, is there another way out, in the workers' movement, when two trends come up, but that of fighting? And when those trends are very divergent, if they oppose one another, is there another way out but secession? Did you ever hear of any other? And is there anything more opposed than revolution and counter-revolution?

For this reason again the KAPD and the General Workers' Unions are quite right.

And, Comrade, have not these secessions, these clearances always been a blessing for the proletariat? Does not this always become evident after a while? I have some experience in this matter. When we as yet belonged to the social-patriotic party we had no influence – after our expulsion we had some – in the beginning, and very soon we won a great, a very great influence. And how about you, the Bolshevists, after the secession? I believe you fared quite well. Small influence at first, very much later on. And all now. It all depends on the economic and political development, whether a group, be it ever so small, does become the most powerful party. If the revolution in Germany lasts, there is a fair hope that the importance and the influence of the workers' unions will surpass all the others. You should not be intimidated by their numbers – 70,000 against seven millions. Smaller groups than these have become the strongest – the Bolshevists, among others!

The industrial unions and workshop organisations, and the Workers' Unions that are based on them and formed from them, why are they such excellent weapons for the revolution in Western Europe, the best weapons even together with the Communist Party? Because the workers act for themselves, infinitely more so than they did in the old Trade Unions, because now they control their leaders, and thereby the entire leadership, and because they have the supervision of the industrial organisation, and thereby of the entire union.

Every trade, every workshop is one whole, where the workers elect their representatives. The industrial organisations have been divided according to economic districts. Representatives have been appointed for the districts. And the districts in turn elect the general board for the entire State.

All the industrial organisations together, no matter to what trade they belong, constitute the one Workers' Union.

This, as we see, is an organisation altogether directed towards the revolution.

If an interval of comparatively peaceful fighting should follow, this organisation might moreover be easily adapted. The industrial organisations would only have to be combined, according to the industries, within the compass of the Workers' Unions.

The Worker has Power.

It is obvious. Here the workers, every worker, has power, for in his workshop he elects his own delegates, and through them he has direct control over the district and State bodies. There is strong centralisation, but not too strong. The individual and the industrial organisation has great power. He can dismiss or replace his delegates at any time, and compel them to replace the higher positions at the shortest notice. This is individualism, but not too much of it. For the central corporations, the districts and government councils have great power. The individual and the central board have just that amount of power, which this present period, in which the revolution breaks out, requires and allows.

Marx writes that under capitalism the citizen is an abstraction, a cipher, as compared to the State. It is the same in the Trade Unions. The bureaucracy, the entire system of the organisation plane ever so far above, and are altogether out of the reach of the worker. He cannot reach them. He is a cipher as compared to them, an abstraction. For them he is not even the man in the workshop. He is not a living, willing, struggling being. If in the old Trade Unions you replace the bureaucracy by other persons, you will see that before long these also have the same character; that they stand high, unattainably high above the masses, and are in no way in touch with them. Ninety-nine out of every hundred will be tyrants, and will stand on the side of the bourgeoisie. It is the very nature of the organisation that makes them so.

Your tactics strive to leave the Trade Unions as they are, "down below," and only to give them other leaders somewhat more of the Left trend, is therefore purely a change "up above." And the Trade Unions remain in *the power of leaders.* And these, once spoilt, everything is as of old, or at the very best, a slight improvement in the layers up above. No, not even if you yourself, or we ourselves, were the leaders, we would not consent to this. For we wish to enable the masses themselves to become more intelligent, more courageous, self-acting, more elevated in all things. We want the masses themselves to make the revolution. For only thus the revolution can triumph here in Western Europe. And to this end the old Trade Unions must be destroyed.

Industrial Workers Decide.

How utterly different it is in the industrial unions. Here it is the worker himself who decides about tactics, trend, and struggle, and who intervenes if the "leaders" do not act as he wants them to. The factory, the workshop, being at the same time the organisation, he stands continually in the fight himself.

In so far as it is possible under capitalism, he is the maker and the guide of his own fate, and as this is the case with every one of them, THE MASS IS THE MAKER AND LEADER OF ITS OWN FIGHT.

More, infinitely more so, than was ever possible in the old Trade Unions, reformist as well as syndicalist (1).

The industrial unions and workers' unions that make the individuals themselves, and consequently the masses themselves, the direct fighters, those that really wage the war, are for that very reason the best weapons for the revolution, the weapons we need here in Western Europe, if ever we shall be able without help to overthrow the most powerful capitalism of the world.

But, Comrade, these are only the weaker grounds yet, as compared to the last, main actual reason, which hangs closely together with the principles I have indicated at the beginning. And it is this last ground which is decisive for the KAPD and the opposition party in England. These parties strive greatly to raise the spiritual level of the masses and individuals in Germany and England.

They are of the opinion that there is only ONE means to that end. And I should like to know whether you know of another means in the Labour movement? It is the formation of a group! That shows, in the struggle, what the mass should be. That shows, fighting, what the mass MUST be. If you know of another means, Comrade, tell me so. I know none other.

In the Labour movement, and especially, I imagine, in the revolution, there is but one way to prove the example – the example itself, the DEED.

The comrades of the Left Wing believe that this small group, in its fight against the Trade Unions and against Capitalism, will win the Trade Unions to its side, or, which is also possible, that gradually the Trade Unions will be directed towards a better course.

This can be attained only through the example. For the raising of the German worker to a higher level, therefore, these new organisations are absolutely indispensable.

The new formation, the Workers' Union, must act

against the Trade Unions, in exactly the same way as the Communist parties act against the Socialist parties (2).

The servile, reformist, social-patriotic masses can be converted only through example.

Next I come to England: to the English Left Wing.

After Germany, England is nearest to a revolution, not because in that country the situation is revolutionary already, but because the proletariat there is so numerous, and the capitalist and economic conditions most favourable. Only a strong blow is needed there and the fight will begin, a fight which can only end in a victory. And the blow will come. This is felt, this is almost instinctively known by the most advanced workers of England (as we all feel it), and because they feel this, they have founded a new movement, which, whilst manifesting itself in various directions, and searching as yet, just as in Germany – is in general the rank and file movement, the movement of the masses themselves, without, or practically without leaders (3).

Their movement is very much like the German Workers' Union and its industrial organisations.

Did you observe, Comrade, that this movement has arisen in two of the most advanced countries only? And from the ranks of the workers themselves? And in many places (4). This proves already in itself that it is of natural growth, and not to be stopped!

Struggle in England Essential.

And in England this movement, this struggle against the Trade Unions, is needed more almost than in Germany, for the English Trade Unions are not only a tool in the hands of the leaders, for the maintenance of capitalism, but they are at the same time far more inefficient as a means for the revolution than those of Germany. The way they are conducted dates from the time of the small struggle, often as far back as the 19th or even the 18th century. England not only has industries where 25 Trade Unions exist, but most of the unions fight one another to the death for members!! And the members are utterly without power. Do you also wish to retain these Trade Unions, Comrade Lenin?

Must not these be opposed, split up, and destroyed? If you are against the Workers' Unions you must also be against the Shop Committees, the Shop Stewards, and the Industrial Unions. Whoever is in favour of the latter, is also in favour of the former. For the Communists in either aim at the same things.

The English Communists of the Left Wing wish to use this new trend in the Trade Union movement to destroy the English Trade Unions in their present shape, to alter them, to replace them by new instruments in the class struggle, which can be applied for the revolution. The same reasons that we have brought forward for the German movement holds good here.

In the postscript of the Executive Committee of the Third International to the KAPD, I have read that the EC is in favour of the IWW in America, as long as this latter wishes only political action and affiliation to the Communist Parties. And these IWW need not join the American Trade Unions! But the Executive Committee is against the Workers' Union in Germany; this latter must join the Trade Unions, although it is communist, and works in cooperation with the political party.

And you, Comrade Lenin, are in favour of the rank and file movement in England (although this often causes a split, and although many of its members want the destruction of the Trade Unions!) and against the Workers' Unions in Germany.

Executive Committee's Opportunism.

I can explain your attitude and that of the Executive Committee only by opportunism; and a mistaken opportunism to boot.

It goes without saying that the Left Wing of the Communists in England cannot go as far as in Germany, because in England the revolution has not begun yet. It cannot as yet organise the rank and file movement all over the country into one whole for the revolution. But the English Left Wing is preparing this. And as soon as the revolution comes, the great masses of workers will leave the old Trade Unions as unserviceable for the revolution, and will join the industrial organisations.

And as the Left Communist Wing penetrates everywhere into this movement, seeking to spread the Communist ideas, it raises the workers by means of its example on to a higher level, also there, and already now. And, as in Germany, that is its real aim (5).

The General Workers' Unions, and the rank and file movement, which are both founded on the factories, the workshops, and on these alone, are the forerunners of the Workers' Councils, the Soviets. As the revolution in Western Europe will be very difficult and consequently of probably very long duration, there will be a long period of transition, in which the Trade Unions are no longer any good, and in which there are no Soviets as yet. This period of transition will be filled out with the struggle against the Trade Unions, their re-forming, their replacing by better organisations. You need not fear, we will have ample time!

Once again this will be so, not because we of the Left Wing will it so, but because the revolution must needs have these new organisations. The revolution cannot triumph without them.

Hail the Rank and File Movement.

All hail, therefore, the rank and file movement in England, and the Workers' Unions in Germany, first forerunners of the Soviets in Europe. Good luck to you, the first organisations that, with the Communist parties, will bring the revolution in Western Europe.

You, Comrade Lenin, wish to compel us to use bad weapons here in Western Europe, where we stand alone, without a single ally, against an as yet extremely powerful, extremely organised and armed capitalism, and where we stand in need of the very best of weapons, the very strongest. Where we want to organise the revolution on the shop floor, and on a shop floor basis, you wish to force the miserable Trade Unions on us. The revolution in Western Europe can and must be organised only on the shop floor and on a shop floor basis, because here capitalism has attained such a high economic and political organisation (in all directions) and because the workers (except for the Communist Party) have no other strong weapons. The Russians were armed, and had the poor peasants. What the weapons and the peasants were for the Russians, tactics and the organisation must be for us for the time being. And then YOU recommend the Trade Unions! From psychological, as well as from material grounds, in the midst of the revolution, we MUST fight these Trade Unions, and you try to hinder us in this fight. We can fight only be means of a splitting-up, and you are preventing us. We wish to form groups, that are to be an example, the only way of showing the proletariat what it is we seek, and you forbid this. We wish to raise the proletariat of Europe to a higher level, and you throw stones in our path.

You do not wish them then: the splitting up, the new formations, the higher stage of development!

And why not?

Because you want to have the big parties, and the big Trade Unions, in the Third International.

To us this looks like opportunism, opportunism of the very worst kind (6).

Today, in the International, your actions differ widely from what they were in the Maximalist party. This was kept very "pure" (and is so to this day, perhaps). In the International, all elements are to be accepted right away, no matter how poorly communistic they are.

It is the curse of the Labour movement that, as soon as it has acquired a certain "power," it seeks to enlarge this power by unprincipled means. Social-Democracy also was originally "pure" in almost all countries. Most social-patriots of today were real Marxists. By Marxist propaganda the masses were won, and as soon as the party gained "power" they were abandoned.

Just as the Social-Democrats acted at that time, you and the Third International are acting now. Not on a national scale, of course, but internationally. The Russian Revolution has triumphed through "purity," through firmness of principle. Now it has gained power, and through it the international proletariat has obtained power, this power is to be extended over Europe, and immediately the old tactics are abandoned!

Instead of applying the same efficacious tactics in ALL the other countries to the inner strengthening of the Third International, opportunism is again resorted to, as before, in Social-Democracy. All elements are now to be affiliated: the Trade Unions, the Independents, the French Centre, parts of the Labour Party. To preserve the semblance of Marxism, conditions are put that have to be SIGNED, and Kautsky, Hilferding, Thomas, etc., are expelled. The great mass, however, the medium quality, is admitted, is driven in by all possible means. And in order that the Centre shall be all the more powerful, the "Left Wing" is not admitted unless it joins that Centre! THE VERY BEST REVOLUTIONARIES, like the KAPD, are excluded!

And when these huge masses have thus been united on one average line, they proceed to one common advance under an iron discipline, and with leaders that have been tested in this most extraordinary manner. A common advance whither? Into the abyss.

Failure of Second International.

What is the use of the finest principles, of the most splendid Theses of the Third International, if in practice we exercise this opportunism? The Second International also had the finest principles, yet it failed *through practice*.

We, however, the Left Wing, refuse to do so. In Western Europe we wish first to build very firm, very clear, and very strong (though at the outset perhaps quite small) parties, kernels, just as you did in Russia. And once we have those, we will make them bigger. But we always want them to be very firm, very strong, very "pure." Only thus can we triumph in Western Europe. Therefore we absolutely reject your tactics, Comrade.

You say that we, the members of the Amsterdam Commission, have forgotten or have never known the lessons former revolutions have taught. Well, Comrade, there is one thing about these former revolutions which I remember quite well. It is this: that the extreme "Left" parties have always played a prominent, eminent part in all of them. It was such in the revolution of the Netherlands against Spain, in the English revolution, in that of France, in the Commune, and in the two Russian revolutions.

In accordance with the development of the Labour movement, there are two trends here in the West-European revolution: the radical and the opportunist trend. These can only arrive at sound tactics, at unity, by means of a mutual struggle. The radical trend, however, though in some particulars it may go too far, is much the best. And yet you, Comrade Lenin, go and support the opportunists!

And not only this! The Executive in Moscow, the RUSSIAN leaders of a revolution that triumphed only through the help of millions of poor peasants, forces these their tactics on the proletariat of Western Europe, which stands and has to stand all alone. And in so doing annihilates the best trend in

Western Europe!

What incredible foolishness, and especially what dialectics:

When the revolution in Western Europe breaks out, it will work for you blue wonders! But the proletariat will be the victim.

Counter-revolutionary Trade Unions.

You, Comrade, and the Executive in Moscow, know that the Trade Unions in Western Europe are counter-revolutionary forces. This is evident from your Theses. And yet you wish to retain them. You also know that the Workers' Union, the rank and file movement, are revolutionary organisations. You say yourself, in your Theses, that the industrial organisations must be and are our aim. And yet you want to smother them. You want to destroy the organisations in which the workers, every worker, and therefore the mass, can attain power and strength, and to keep those in which the mass is a dead tool in the hands of the leaders. Thus you strive to bring the Trade Unions in your power, in the power of the Third International.

Why is it you wish to do so? Why do you follow these bad tactics? Because you want masses around you, no matter of what quality, as long as they are masses. Because you believe that if only you have masses obeying you on account of a strict discipline and centralisation, no matter whether they are communist, half communist, or not communist at all, you, the leaders, will win, in a word, because your tactics are leader-tactics.

By criticizing leader-tactics I do not mean to advocate politics without leaders and centralisation, for without these one attains nothing (they are as indispensable as the party). I am criticizing those politics that collect masses, without inquiring into their convictions, their heart; politics that assume that the leaders, once they have great masses around them, will be able to win.

Russian Tactics Useless in Western Europe.

But these politics, which you and the Executive are now following, will lead nowhere in Western Europe. Capitalism here is far too powerful as yet, and the proletariat is much too isolated. These politics will fail here, just as those of the Second International did.

Here the workers themselves must become strong, and, through them, their leaders. Here the evil the leadership-policy, must be seized by the root

Through these your tactics on the Trade Union question you and the Moscow Executive have proved, to my mind, that UNLESS YOU ALTER THESE TACTICS, YOU CANNOT CONDUCT THE REVOLUTION IN WESTERN EUROPE.

You say that the Left Wing, in following its tactics, can only talk. Well, Comrade, in the other countries the Left Wing has had next to no opportunities as yet to act. But look at Germany, and the tactics and actions of the KAPD in the "Kapp putsch" and with regard to the Russian revolution, and you will have to take those words back.

NOTES

1. It has to be borne in mind, of course, that this new combination of individualism and centralism is not given right away in its completed form, but that it is only springing up now, and is a process, which will be developed only in the struggle itself, and thus perfected.

2. With the sarcastic remark that also the Workers' Union cannot be faultless, you make little impression. It is right only in so far that the union must fight for reforms under capitalism. It is not right in so far as the union fights for the revolution.

3. Shop Committees, Shop Stewards, and, especially in Wales, Industrial Unions.

4. That this movement in Germany was made from above is slander.

5. You, Comrade, and many with you, use here the argument that the Communists, by leaving the Trade Unions, lose touch with the masses. But is not the closest touch obtained in the workshops? And have not all workshops turned more than ever into debating halls? How can the Left Communists possibly lose touch, then?

6. Already now the Trade Union question clearly demonstrates where the opportunist tactics of Moscow lead. The members of the Communist Parties are forced to enter the modern Trade Unions (see the thesis accepted on this point). They are forced, therefore, to become scabs and strike-breakers!!! At the same time they must openly support the Syndicalists!!! Instead of openly saying that neither of these organisations are any good, that new ones have to be formed, on the basis of the industries (the theses themselves declare elsewhere that this is what should be done), they adopt this ambiguous attitude. And why? To add masses to the Third International.

Parliamentarism

Subjects of Bourgeois Democracy.

In the first place, the workers of Western Europe and the working masses in general are completely subjected, as far as ideas are concerned, to the bourgeois system of representation, to parliamentarism, to bourgeois democracy. Much more so than the workers of Eastern Europe. Here bourgeois ideology has taken a strong hold on the whole of social and political life. It has penetrated far more into the heads and hearts of the workers. Here they have already been brought up in that ideology for hundreds of years. These ideas have altogether saturated the workers.

These relations have been very well depicted by Comrade Pannekoek in the Viennese periodical, *Kommunismus*:

"The experience of Germany places us face to face with the great problem of the revolution in Western Europe. In these countries the old bourgeois method of production, and the corresponding highly developed culture of many centuries, have made a thorough impression on the thoughts and feelings of the masses. Consequently the spiritual and mental character of the masses here is quite different from that of the Eastern countries, where they had not experienced this domination of bourgeois culture. And herein above all lies the difference in the progress of the revolution in the East and in the West. In England, France, Holland, Scandinavia, Italy and Germany, ever since the middle ages there has been a strong bourgeoisie, with petty-bourgeois and primitive capitalist production; whilst feudalism was being defeated, an equally strong, independent peasantry sprang up in the country, which was master in its own small sphere.

On this soil bourgeois civic spiritual life developed into a firm national culture, especially in the coastlands of England and France, which were most advanced by capitalist development. In the nineteenth century capitalism, by bringing the whole of agriculture under its power, and pulling even the most isolated farms into the circle of the world economy, has raised this national culture to a higher level, has refined it, and by means of its spiritual methods of propaganda, the Press, the school, and the Church, has beaten it firmly into the brains of the masses it has proletarianised, both those who were sucked into the cities, and those who were left on the land. This applies not only to the original capitalist countries, but also, though in a somewhat modified form, to America and Australia, where the Europeans founded new States, and to the countries of Central Europe, that had until then stagnated: Germany, Austria, Italy, where new capitalist development could link up with old, obsolete, petty- bourgeois economy, agriculture and culture. In the Eastern countries of Europe capitalism found quite different material and other traditions. Here in Russia, Poland, Hungary, and the region to the east of the Elbe, there was no small, strong bourgeois class dominating spiritual life since time immemorial; primitive agrarian relations with large scale landed property, patriarchal feudalism and village communism determined spiritual life.

Here, on the ideological problem, Comrade Pannekoek has hit the nail on the head. Far better than it has ever been done from your side, he has demonstrated the difference between the east and the west of Europe, from the ideological angle, and has given the cue towards finding revolutionary tactics for Western Europe.

This only need be combined with the MATERIAL causes of the power of our opponents, that is to say with banking capital, and the tactics become perfectly clear.

Workers Win Rights for Possessing Class.

However, there is yet more to be said on the ideological question: civil liberties, the power of parliament, has been won in Western Europe by means of wars for liberty, waged by former generations, by the ancestors. And though at the time these rights were only for citizens, for the possessing class, they were won by the people all the same. The thought of these struggles is to this day a deeply-rooted tradition in the blood of this people. Revolutions are always the deepest memories of a people. Unconsciously the thought that it meant a victory to achieve representation in parliament has a tremendous, silent force. This is especially the case in the oldest bourgeois countries, where long or repeated wars have been waged for freedom: in England, Holland and France. Also, though on a smaller scale, in Germany, Belgium, and the Scandinavian countries. An inhabitant of the East cannot realise, perhaps, how strong this influence can be.

Moreover the workers themselves have fought here, often for years, for universal suffrage, and have thus obtained it, directly or indirectly. This was also a victory, which bore fruit at the time. The thought and the feeling generally prevails, that it is progress, and a victory, to be represented, and to entrust one's representative with the care of one's affairs in Parliament. The influence of this ideology is enormous.

And finally, reformism has brought the working class of Western Europe altogether under the power of the parliamentary representatives, who have led it into war, and into alliances with capitalism. The influence of reformism is also colossal.

All these causes have made the worker the slave of Parliament, to which he leaves all action. He himself does not act any longer (2).

Then comes the revolution. Now he has to act *for* himself. Now the worker, alone with his class, must fight the gigantic enemy, must wage the most terrible fight that ever was.

No tactics of the leaders can help him. Desperately the classes, all classes, oppose the workers, and not one class sides with them. On the contrary, if he should trust his leaders, or other classes in parliament, he runs a great risk of falling back into his old weakness of letting the leaders act for him, of trusting parliament, of persevering in the old notion that others can make the revolution for him, of pursuing illusions, of remaining in the old bourgeois ideology.

This relationship of the masses to the leaders has also been excellently characterised by Comrade Pannekoek:

"Parliamentarism is the typical form of the kind of fight carried out by means of leaders, in which the masses themselves play but a minor part. Its practice consists in this: that representatives, individual persons, carry on the actual fighting. With the masses it must therefore awaken the illusion that others can do the fighting for them. Formerly the belief was that the leaders could obtain important reforms for the workers through parliament; many had even had the illusion that the members of parliament, by means of laws and regulations, could carry out the transition to Socialism. Today, since parliamentarism acts in a more honest way, the argument is heard that the representatives may do great things in parliament for communist propaganda. Ever again the importance of the leaders is emphasised, and it is only natural that professionals should decide about politics, be it in the democratic guise of congress discussions and resolutions. The history of Social Democracy is a series of fruitless attempts to let the members determine their own politics. Wherever the proletariat goes in for parliamentary action, all this is inevitable, as long as the masses have not yet created organs for self-activity; as long, therefore, as the revolution has not broken out. As soon as the masses can act for themselves, and can consequently decide, the disadvantages of parliamentarism become paramount.

The problem of tactics is how to eradicate the traditional bourgeois way of thinking that saps the strength of the mass of the proletariat; everything which reinforces the traditional view is wrong. The most firmly rooted, most tenacious part of this mental attitude is dependence on leaders, to whom it leaves the decisions in all general questions, and the control of all class matters. Inevitably, parliamentarism has a tendency to crush in the masses the activity necessary for the revolution. No matter what fine speeches are delivered to inspire the workers to revolutionary deeds, revolutionary action does not spring from such words, but from the keen and hard necessity that leaves no other choice whatsoever.

Demands of the Revolution.

The revolution also demands something more than the fighting action of the masses that overthrows the government, and which, as we know, is not under the control of leaders, but can only come from the deeply felt impulse of the masses. The revolution demands that the great questions of social construction be taken in hand, that difficult decisions shall be made, that the entire proletariat be roused to one creative impulse; and this is only possible if first the advance guard, and then an ever greater mass takes things in hand – a mass that is conscious of its responsibilities, that searches, propagates, fights, strives, reflects, considers, dares, and carries out. All this is, however, hard work: so as long as the proletariat thinks there is an easier way, letting others act for it by carrying out agitation from a high platform, by taking decisions, by giving signals for action, by making laws, it will hesitate, and the old ways of thinking and the old weaknesses will keep them pacified.

The workers of Western Europe, let it be repeated a thousand and, if need be, a hundred thousand or a million times – and whoever has not learned and seen it since November 1918 is blind – the West European workers must in the first place act for themselves – in the Trade Unions and also politically, and they must let their leaders act, because the workers stand alone, and because no clever tactics of leaders can help them. The greatest impetus must come from them. Here, for the first time, to a far greater degree than in Russia, THE LIBERATION OF THE WORKERS MUST BE THE WORK OF THE WORKERS THEMSELVES. That is why comrades of the Left Wing are right in saying to the German Comrades: don't participate in the elections, and boycott parliament – politically you must do everything for yourselves – you cannot win unless you do so for two, five, or ten years; unless you train yourself to it man by man, group after group, from town to town, from province to province, and finally in the entire land, as a party, a union; as industrial councils, as a mass, and as a class. You cannot win unless finally, through incessant training and fighting, and through defeat, you advance to that stage, the great majority among you, where you can do all this, and where, at last, after all this schooling, you constitute one united mass.

And that is why the comrades of the KAPD were right, perfectly right – history demanded it of them – at once to proceed to a secession, to split the Trade Unions; as this covers the entire political question, there is an urgent need for the fight, the example, the lead.

An Example Needed.

But these comrades of the Left Wing, the KAPD, would have committed a grave mistake had they done nothing but preach and propagate this. Here even more perhaps, than in the case of the party, when the Spartakus League, or rather the Spartakus Zentrale, refused to stand this propaganda of theirs. For what the German slaves, what all workers of Western Europe needed in the first place, was an example. In this nation of political slaves, and in this subjected West European world, there had to be a group that gave the example of free fighters without leaders, that is to say, without leaders of the old type – without members of parliament.

And once again all this must be, not because it is so beautiful, or good, or heroic, but because the German and West-

European proletariat stands alone in this terrible fight, without help from any other class, because the cleverness of the leaders is of no avail any longer, because there is but one thing that is needed, the will and firmness of the mass, man for man, woman for woman, and of the mass as a whole.

For this higher motive, and because the opposite tactics, parliamentary action, can but harm this higher cause, infinitely higher than the petty profit of parliamentary propaganda, for this higher motive the Left Wing rejects parliamentarism.

You say that Comrade Liebknecht, if he yet lived, might work wonders in the Reichstag. We deny it. Politically he could not manoeuvre there, because all the bourgeois parties oppose us in one united front. And he could win the workers no better in parliament than outside it. On the other hand, the masses, to a very great extent, would leave everything to be done through his speeches, so that his parliamentary action would have a harmful effect (3).

Big Numbers of no Avail.

It is true that this work of the Left Wing would take years, and those people who for some reason or other, strive for immediate results, big numbers, large amounts of members and votes, big parties, and a powerful (seemingly powerful!) International, will have a rather long time to wait. Those, however, who realise that the victory of the German and West-European revolution can only come, if a very great number, if the mass of the workers believe in themselves, will be satisfied with these tactics.

For Germany and Western Europe they are the only tactics possible. This is particularly true for England.

Comrade, do you know the bourgeois individualism of England, its bourgeois liberty, its parliamentary democracy, as they have grown during some six or seven centuries? Do you really know them? Do you know how utterly they differ from conditions in your country? Do you know how deeply these ideas are rooted in everyone, also in the proletarian individuals of England and its colonies? Do you know into what an immense whole it has developed? Do you know how generally spread it is? In social and personal life? I do not think there is one Russian, one inhabitant of Eastern Europe, who knows them. If you knew them, you would rejoice at those among the English workers who totally break with this greatest political formation of world capitalism.

If this is done with full consciousness, it demands a revolutionary mind, quite as great as that which once broke with Czarism. This rupture with the entire English democracy constitutes the era of the English revolution.

And this is done, as it must inevitably be done in England, with its tremendous history, tradition, and strength; it is done with the utmost firmness of purpose. Because the English proletariat has the greatest power (potentially it is the most powerful on the earth), it makes a sudden stand against the mightiest bourgeoisie of the earth, and with one stroke rejects the whole of English democracy, although the revolution has not yet broken out there.

That is what their vanguard did, just like the German one, the KAPD. And why did they do it? Because they know that they also stand alone, and that no class in all England will help them, and that above all the proletariat itself, and not the leaders, must fight and win there (4).

A Great Day.

It was an historic day, Comrade, when on this June day in London the first Communist Party was founded, and this Party rejected the entire structure and government apparatus of seven hundred years. I wish Marx and Engels could have been present there. I believe they would have felt a great, a supreme joy at seeing how these English workers rejected the English State, the example for all States of the earth, and which for centuries has been the centre and stronghold of world capitalism and rules over one third of humanity; how they reject it and its parliament, though only theoretically as yet.

These tactics are all the more necessary in England because English capitalism supports the capitalism of all other countries, and will decidedly not scruple to summon auxiliaries from all over the world, against every foreign, as well as against its own proletariat. The fight of the English proletariat, therefore, is a struggle against world capitalism. All the more reason for the English Communists to give the most elevated and brilliant example. To wage an exemplary fight on behalf of the world proletariat, and to strengthen it by example (5).

Thus there has to be everywhere one group that draws all the consequences; such groups are the salt of humanity.

Here, however, after this theoretical defence of anti-parliamentarism, I have to answer in detail your defence of parliamentarism. You defend it (from page 36 to 68), for England and Germany. The argumentation, however, holds good only for Russia (and at the very utmost for a few other East-European countries), not for Western Europe. That, as I have said before, IS Where your mistake lies. That turns you from a Marxist into an opportunist leader. That causes you, the Marxist, radical leader for Russia, and probably a few more East-European countries, to sink back into opportunism where Western Europe is concerned. And, if accepted here, your tactics would lead the entire West to perdition. This I will next prove in detail, in answer to your argumentation.

Comrade, on reading your agumentation from page 36 to 68, a recollection constantly occurred to me.

Amongst the Social Patriots.

I saw myself once more at a congress of the old Social-Patriotic Party of Holland, listening to a speech of Troelstra's – a speech in which he depicted to the workers the great advantages of the reformist policy, in which he spoke of the workers that were not social-democratic yet, and that were to be won by compromise; in which he spoke of the alliances that were to be made (only provisionally, of course!) with the parties of these workers, and of the "rifts" in and between the bourgeois parties, of which we were to make use. In just the same way, in almost, nay in absolutely the same words, you, Comrade Lenin, speak for us West Europeans!

And I remember how we sat there, far back in the hall; we the Marxist Comrades, very few in number – only four or five. Henriette Roland Holst, Pannekoek, and a few others. Troelstra spoke persuasively and convincingly, just as you do, Comrade. And I remember how, in the midst of the thundering applause, of the brilliant reformist expositions and the reviling of Marxism, the workers in the hall looked round at the "idiots" and "asses" and "childish fools," names that Troelstra called us at that time – almost the same as you call us now. To all probability things have been practically the same at the Congress of the International in Moscow, when you spoke against the "Left" Marxists. And his words – just like yours, Comrade – were so convincing, so logical, within the compass of his method, that at times *I* myself thought, yes, he is right.

Usually I was the one to speak for the opposition (in the years up to 1909, when we were expelled). Shall I tell you what I did, when I began to doubt about myself? I had a means that never failed: it was a sentence from the Party Programme:

"You shall ever act or speak in such a way that the class consciousness of the workers shall be roused and strengthened."

And I asked myself: is the class consciousness of the workers roused or not by what the man over there is saying? And then I always knew that at once this was not the case, and that therefore I was right.

It was just the same reading your brochure. I hear your opportunist arguments for cooperation with non-Communist parties, with bourgeois elements, for compromise. And I am carried away. It all seems so brilliant, clear and fine. And so logical as well. But then I consider, as I used to long ago, just one phrase which some time ago I made for myself, for the campaign against the Communist opportunists. It is as follows:

Is what yonder Comrade says the sort of thing that strengthens the will of the masses for action, for the revolution, for the real revolution in Western Europe – yes or no?

And with regard to your brochure, my head and heart answer at the same time: no. Then I know at once, as surely as one can possibly know anything, that you are wrong.

I can recommend this method to the comrades of the Left Wing. Whenever you want to know, Comrades, in the severe struggles ahead of us, against the opportunists of all countries (here in Holland they have been waging for the last three years) whether and why you are right, ask yourself this question!

Lenin's Three Arguments.

In your opposition to us, Comrade, you use only three arguments, that constantly recur all through your brochure, either separately or combined.

They are the following:

1. The advantages of parliamentary propaganda for winning the workers and the petit bourgeois elements to our side.

2. The advantages of parliamentary action for making use of the "rifts" between the parties, and for compromises with some of them.

3. The example of Russia, where this propaganda and the compromise worked so wonderfully well.

Further arguments you have none; I will answer them in turn.

55

To begin with the first argument, propaganda in parliament. This argument is only of very slight importance, for the non-communist workers, that is to say the social-democrats the Christian and other bourgeois elements do not, as a rule, read one word in their papers about *our* parliamentary speeches

Often these speeches are utterly mutilated. With those, therefore, we achieve nothing We only get at the workers through our meetings, brochures and newspapers

Action Speaks Louder than Words.

We, however (I often speak in the name of the KAPD), get at them especially through action (in the time of the revolution of which we speak) In all bigger towns and villages they see us act. They see our strikes, our street fights our councils. They hear our watchwords. They see our lead. This is the best propaganda, the most convincing. This action, however, is not in parliament!

The non-communist workers, therefore, the small peasants and bourgeois, can be reached quite well also without parliamentary action

Here one part in particular from your brochure *Infantile Disorder*, must be refuted; it shows where opportunism is already leading you, Comrade.

On page 52 you say that the fact of the German workers coming in masses to join the ranks of the Independent Party, and not the Communist Party, is attributable to the parliamentary action of the Independents. The mass of the Berlin workers, therefore, had been as good as converted through the death of our Comrades Liebknecht and Rosa Luxemburg, through the purposeful strikes and the street fights of the Communists. Only a speech of Comrade Levi in parliament was lacking as yet! Had he but delivered this speech, they would have come to us, instead of to the double-minded Independents! No, comrade, this is not true. They have gone to the double-minds first because they were afraid as yet of the single-minded: the revolution. Because the transition from slavery to freedom lies through hesitation.

Look out, Comrade, you see whither opportunism is already leading you.

Your first argument is of no importance.

And if we consider that parliamentary action (in the revolution, in Germany and England, and all Western Europe) reinforces the workers' idea that their leaders will do things for them, and dissuades them from the idea that they must do everything for themselves, we see that this argument does not only bring no good at all, but that it is exceedingly harmful.

The second argument: the advantage of parliamentary action (in revolutionary periods) for taking advantage of the rifts between the parties, and for compromises with some of them.

An Uncongenial Task.

To refute this argument (especially for England and Germany, but also for all Western Europe), I shall have to go somewhat more into detail than with .the first. It is most uncongenial to me, Comrade, that I should have to do this against you. This entire question of revolutionary opportunism, for it is no longer reformist, but revolutionary opportunism, is a vital question, literally a matter of life and death for us West-Europeans. The matter itself, the refutation, is easy. We have refuted this argument a hundred times, when Troelstra, Henderson, Bernstein, Legien, Renaudel, Van der Velde, etc., all the Social-Patriots, used it. Why Kautsky, when he was still Kautsky, has refuted it. It was the greatest argument of the reformists. We did not think we would ever have to do it against you. Now we have to.

Well then: The advantage of profiting in parliament from the "rifts" is utterly insignificant, for the very reason that for several years, for a score of years, these "rifts" have been insignificant. Those between the big bourgeois and the petty-bourgeois parties. In Western Europe, in Germany and England. This does not date from the revolution. It was so long before, in the period of peaceful evolution. All parties, including the petty-bourgeoisie and the small peasants, had been AGAINST the workers for a long time already, and between themselves the difference in matters concerning the workers (and consequently on nearly all points), had become very slight, or had often quite disappeared.

This is an established fact, theoretically as well as practically, in Western Europe, in Germany and England.

Theoretically, because capital concentrates in banks, trusts, and monopolies to an enormous degree.

In Western Europe, and especially in England and Germany, these banks, trusts and cartels have assimilated nearly all capital in the industries, commerce, transport, and to a great extent even in agriculture. The whole of industry, including small scale industry, the whole of transport, including the small enterprises, the whole of commerce, big as well as small, and the greater part of agriculture, big and small, has consequently become absolutely dependent on big capital. They have fused with it.

Comrade Lenin says that small commerce, transport, industry and agriculture, waver between capital and workers. This is wrong. It was so in Russia, and it used to be so here. In Western Europe, in Germany and England, they are now so largely, so utterly dependent on big capital, that they no longer waver. The small shop owner, the small industrialist, the small trader, are absolutely in the power of the trusts, the monopolies, the banks. It is from these that they get their goods and credit. And even the small peasant, through his cooperative and his mortgages, is dependent on the trust, the monopoly, and the banks.

Comrade, this part of my argumentation, the argumentation of the "Left Wing," is the most important of all. The entire tactics for Europe and America depend on it.

What elements do they consist of, Comrade, these lower layers that stand nearest to the proletariat? Of shop owners, artisans, lower officials and employees, and poor peasants.

Let us consider what these are in Western Europe! Follow me, Comrade. Not only in a big shop – there the dependence on capital is a matter of course – but in a small one in a poor, proletarian quarter. Look around you. What do you see? Everything: nearly all the goods, clothes, foodstuffs, implements, fuel etc., are products not only of big industry, but often of the trusts. And not only in the cities, but in the country likewise. The small shopkeepers are for the most part storekeepers of big capital. That is to say of banking capital, for this rules the large factories and the trusts.

Look about you in the workshop of a small artisan, no matter whether in the city or the country. His raw materials, the metals, the leather, the wood, etc., come to him from big capital, often even from the monopolies, that is to say from the banks as well. And in so far as the purveyors are small capitalists as yet, these in their turn depend on banking capital.

And the lower officials and employees? The great majority of them in Western Europe is in the employment of big capital, the State, of the municipality, finally therefore also of the banks. The percentage of employees and officials nearest to the proletariat that are directly or indirectly dependent on big capital is very great in Western Europe. In Germany and England, as well as in the United States and the British colonies, it is enormous.

And the interests of these layers are one therefore with those of big capital, that is to say the banks.

I have already dealt with the poor peasants, and we have seen, that for the time being they cannot be won for

59

Communism, for the reasons already mentioned, and also because they are dependent on big capital for their implements, goods, and mortgages.

What does this prove, Comrade?

That modern West-European (and American) society and State have become ONE big, thoroughly organised whole, which is entirely controlled, moved and regulated by banking capital. That society here is a regulated body, capitalistically regulated, but regulated all the same. That banking capital is the blood, flowing through the entire body, and nourishing all its branches. That this body is one, and that capital renders this body enormously strong, and that therefore all the members will stand by it to the very end – all except the proletariat, which makes this blood: surplus value.

Through this dependence of all classes on banking capital and through the enormous strength of banking capital, all the classes are hostile to the revolution, so that the proletariat stands alone.

And as banking capital is the most pliable and elastic force in the world, and increases its power a thousand times through its credit, it upholds and maintains capitalism and the capitalist State, even after this terrible war, after the loss of thousands of billions, and in the midst of conditions that seem like bankruptcy to us.

And it is through this that, with all the more force, it collects all classes around it, combining them into one whole, against the proletariat. And the force and pliability, and the unison of all classes are so great, that they will last long after the revolution has broken out.

Cause of Revolution's Delay.

It is true that capital has been terribly weakened. The crisis is coming, and with it the revolution. And I believe that the revolution will win. But there are two things that still keep capitalism very strong: the spiritual slavery of the masses, and banking capital.

Our tactics, therefore, have to be based on the power of these two things.

And there is one other cause through which organised banking capital rallies all the classes against the revolution. It is the great number of proletarians. All the classes feel that if only they could induce the workers (in Germany alone almost twenty million) to work 10, 12, or 14 hours a day, then there would be a way out of the crisis. That is why they hold together.

These are the economic conditions in Western Europe.

In Russia banking capital did not have this power yet, so there the bourgeoisie and the lower classes did not unite. Consequently, there were real rifts between them. And there the proletariat did not stand alone.

These economic causes determine politics. It is through this that those classes in Western Europe (dependent slaves that they are) vote for their masters, for these big capitalist parties, and that they belong to them. In Germany and England, in Western Europe, these elements have hardly any parties of their own.

All this was very strong already before the revolution and before the war. Now through the war it has become intensified to an enormous extent – through nationalism and chauvinism, but especially through the massive trustification of all economic forces. Through the revolution, however, this tendency – unity of all bourgeois parties with all petty-bourgeois elements and all poor peasants – has again been immensely strengthened.

The Russian Revolution has not been in vain! Now we know everywhere what to expect.

Thus in Western Europe, and especially in England and

Germany, the big bourgeoisie and the big peasants, the middle classes and middle peasants, the lower bourgeoisie and the small peasants, are all united against the workers, through monopoly, the banks, the trusts; through imperialism, the war and revolution (6). And, as the labour question encompasses all things, they are united on all questions.

Here, Comrade, I must make the same remark I have already made (in the first chapter) with regard to the peasant question. I know quite well that the little minds in our Party, that lack the strength to base tactics on great, general lines, and consequently base them on the small, particular ones, that these little minds will call the attention to those elements among these layers, that have not yet come under the banner of big capital.

I do not deny that there are such elements, but I maintain that the general truth, the general tendency in Western Europe, is that they are under the banner of big capital. And it is on this general truth that our tactics must be based!

Neither do I deny that there may be "rifts" yet. I only say that the general tendency is, and will be, for a long time after the revolution: unity of these classes. And I say that for the workers in Western Europe it is better to have their attention directed to that unity than to these rifts. For it is they themselves that must in the first place make the revolution, and not their leaders, their Members of Parliament.

Nor do I say that (which the little minds will make of my words) that the real interests of these classes are the same as those of big capital. I know that these classes are oppressed by it.

What I say is simply this:

These classes cling to big capital even more firmly than before, because now they also see the danger of the proletarian revolution ahead.

In Western Europe the domination of capital means to them a more or less sure existence, the possibility of, or at least the belief in, a betterment of their position. Now they are threatened by chaos and the revolution, which for some time to come means worse chaos. That is why they side with capital in the effort to sweep chaos away by every possible means, to save production, to drive the workers to work longer hours, and to endure privation patiently. For them the proletarian revolution in Western Europe is the fall and breakdown of all order, of all security of existence, be it ever so insufficient. Therefore they all support big capital, and will continue to do so for a long time, including during the revolution.

All Classes Fight the Proletariat.

For finally I must yet point out that what I have said applies to the tactics at the beginning and in the course of the revolution. I know that quite at the end of the revolution, when victory draws near and capitalism has been shattered, these classes will come to us. But we must determine our tactics not for the end, but for the beginning and in the course of the revolution.

Theoretically, therefore, all this had to be so.

Theoretically these classes had to cooperate.

Theoretically this is an established fact. But practically as well.

This I will prove next:

For many years already the entire bourgeoisie, all bourgeois parties in Western Europe, also those that belong to the small peasants and middle bourgeoisie, have done nothing for the workers. And they were all of them hostile to the labour movement, and in favour of imperialism, in favour of the war.

For years already there had not been a single party in England, in Germany, in Western Europe, that supported the workers. All were opposed to them; in all matters (7).

There was no new labour legislation. Conditions grew

63

worse instead. Laws were passed against going on strike. Even higher taxes were levied.

Imperialism, colonisation, marinism and militarism were supported by all bourgeois, including the petty-bourgeois parties. The difference between liberal and clerical, conservative and progressive, big and petty bourgeois, disappeared.

Everything which the social-patriots, the reformists said, about the difference between the parties, about the "rifts" between them, was a fraud. And all this has now been brought forward by you, Comrade Lenin! It was a fraud for all countries in Western Europe. This has been best proved in July-August 1914.

At that time they were all one. And the revolution has made them even far more united in practice. Against the revolution, and consequently against all workers, for the revolution alone can bring actual betterment to all workers, against the revolution they all stand together without a single "rift."

And as through the war, the crisis and the revolution, all social and political questions have come to be connected in practice with the question of the revolution, these classes in Western Europe stand together in all questions, and in opposition to the proletariat.

In a word, the trust, the monopoly, the big banks, imperialism, the war, the revolution, have in practice riveted together into one class all the West-European big and petty bourgeois and peasant parties against the workers (8).

Theoretically and practically, therefore, this is an established fact. In the revolution in Western Europe and especially in England and Germany, there are no "rifts" of any considerable importance between these classes.

Here again I must add something personal. On pages 40 and 41 you criticise the Amsterdam Bureau. You cite a thesis of the bureau. Parenthetically, what you say with regard to this is wrong – all of it. But you also say that the Amsterdam Commission, before condemning parliamentarism, ought to have given an analysis of the class relations and the political parties, to justify this condemnation. Excuse me, Comrade, this was not the task of the Commission. For that on which their thesis is based, to wit that all bourgeois parties in Parliament as well as more outside, had been all along, and were even now, opposed to the workers, and did not show the slightest "rift," all this had been ascertained long ago, and was an established fact for all Marxists. In Western Europe at any rate, there was no need for us to analyse that.

On the contrary, considering you strive for compromise and alliances in Parliament, which would lead us into opportunism, it was your duty to demonstrate that there are any rifts of importance between the bourgeois parties.

You wish to lead us, here in Western Europe, into compromising. What Troelstra, Henderson, Scheidemann, Turati, etc., could not accomplish in the time of evolution, you wish to do during the revolution. It is for you to prove that this can be done.

Opposing Capitalist Forces Unite to Defeat Revolution.

And this not by means of Russian examples; these are easy enough, to be sure, but with West-European examples. This duty you have fulfilled in the most miserable way. No wonder you took almost exclusively your Russian experience, that of a very backward country, not that of the Western Europe of these modern days.

In the entire booklet, in the parts which deal with these very questions of tactics, the Russian examples excepted, to which I will soon proceed, I find but two examples from Western Europe, the Kapp putsch in Germany, and the Lloyd George-Churchill government in England, with the opposition of Asquith.

Very few examples indeed, and of the poorest quality, that there are "rifts" between the bourgeois, and in this case also the social democratic parties!

If ever a proof was needed that between the bourgeois (and in this case also the social democratic parties), there are no important rifts as regards the workers, in the revolution, and here in Western Europe; the Kapp putsch furnishes that proof. The Kappites did not punish, kill and imprison the democrats, the Zentrum people, and the social democrats. And when these came into power again, they did not punish, kill and imprison the Kappites. But both parties killed the Communists!

Communism was too weak as yet. That is why they did not TOGETHER forge a dictatorship. Next time, when Communism will be stronger, they will organise a dictatorship BETWEEN THEM.

It was and is your duty, Comrade, to point out in what way the Communists could at that time have taken advantage in Parliament of that rift – in such a way, of course, as to benefit the workers. It was and is your duty to tell us what the Communist Members of Parliament ought to have said to make the workers see this rift, and take advantage of it – in such a way, of course, as not to strengthen the bourgeois parties. You cannot do this, because during the revolution there is no rift of any importance. And it is of the time of the revolution that we speak. And it was your duty to point out that if in special cases there should be such rifts, it would be more advantageous to direct the attention of the workers in that direction than to the general tendency towards unity.

And it was and is your duty, Comrade, before beginning to lead us in Western Europe, to show where those rifts are, in England, in Germany, in Western Europe.

This you cannot do either. You speak of a rift between Churchill, Lloyd George, and Asquith, of which the workers are to take advantage. This is altogether pitiful. I will not even discuss this with you. For everyone knows that since in England the industrial proletariat has some power, these rifts have been artificially made by the bourgeois parties and leaders and are yet being made, to mislead the workers, to entice them from the one side to the other, and back again ad infinitum, thus to keep them for ever powerless and dependent. To this end they even at times admit two opponents to the one government, Lloyd George and Churchill. And Comrade Lenin lets himself be caught in this trap, that is well nigh a century old! He strives to induce the British workers to base their politics on this fraud! At the time of the revolution, the Churchills, Lloyd George, and the Asquiths will unite against the revolution, and then you, Comrade, will have betrayed and weakened the English proletariat with an illusion. It was your duty to point out not by means of general, fine and brilliant figures of speech (as in the entire last chapter, on page 72 for instance), but accurately, concretely, by means of clear examples and facts, what those conflicts and differences are – not the Russian ones, nor those that are of no importance, or artificially made, but by means of the actual, important, West-European examples. This you do nowhere in your brochure. And as long as you do not give these, we do not believe you. When you give them we will answer you – until then we say: it is nothing but illusions that mislead the workers, and lead them into false tactics. The truth is, Comrade, that you wrongly assume the West-European and the Russian revolutions to be alike. And for what reason? Because you forget that in the modern, that is to say the West-European and North American States, there is a power that stands above the various kinds of capitalists – the landowners, industrial magnates, and merchants banking capital. This power, which is identical with imperialism, unites all capitalists, including the small peasants and bourgeois.

One thing, however, remains to you. You say there are rifts between Labour parties and the bourgeois parties, and that these can be made use of. That is right.

We might aver, to be sure, that these differences between

the social democrats and bourgeois in the war and in the revolution have been very slight and have disappeared in most cases! But they might be there. And they may arise yet. Of those we must therefore speak. Especially as you put it, the "pure" English Labour government, Thomas, Henderson, Clynes, etc., in England, against Sylvia Pankhurst, and the possibly "pure" socialist government of Ebert, Scheidemann, Noske, Hilferding, Crispien, Cohn, against the KAPD (10).

You say that your tactics, which direct the workers' attention towards these Labour governments, encouraged them to promote their formation, are clear and effective; whilst ours, which are opposed to their formation, are harmful.

No, Comrade, our attitude with regard to these cases of "pure" Labour government where the rift between these parties of workers and those of the bourgeoisie became a split, is again quite clear, and profitable, to the revolution.

It is possible that we shall allow such a government to exist. It can be necessary, it can mean progress for the movement. If this is so, we cannot proceed any further yet, we will let it exist, criticising them as keenly as possible, and replace them by a Communist government as soon as we can. But to promote its arrival in Parliament and in elections, this will not do in Western Europe.

And we will not do this, because in Western Europe and in the revolution the workers stand all alone. For that reason everything – do you understand this? – everything HERE depends on their will for action, on their clearness of brain. And because of these, your tactics of compromising with the Scheidemanns and Hendersons, with the Crispiens and their followers among the English Independents, of the opportunist Communists of the Spartacus League or the BSP – because these tactics inside and outside Parliament confuse heads, here in Western Europe and in the revolution – making the workers elect someone whom they know beforehand to be an impostor, and because our tactics on the other hand make them clear-sighted, by showing them the enemy as enemy, because of all this and, even at the risk of losing a representative in Parliament in periods of illegality, or of missing the benefit, of a "rift" (in Parliament!), we in Western Europe, and under the present conditions, choose our tactics and reject yours.

Here again your advice leads to confusion, and awakens illusions.

But what about the members of the social democratic parties, the German Independents, the Labour Party, and the Independent Party? Must not those be won?

These, the working class and petty-bourgeois elements among them, will be won by us, the Left Wing, in Western Europe, through our propaganda, our meetings and our press, and especially through our example, our slogans, our action on the shop floor. In the revolution, those who are not won thus, through our action, through the revolution, are lost anyway, and can go to the devil. These social-democratic, Independent Labour Parties in England and Germany consist of workers and petty-bourgeois elements. The first, the workers, can all be won in the long run. The petty-bourgeois elements only to a very slight extent, and are of little economic importance; these few will be won over by our propaganda, etc.. The majority of them – and it is on these that Noske and his conjurers rely above all – belong to capitalism, and, in proportion to the revolution's advance, they rally all the closer around it.

Workshop, not Parliament, the Battle-ground.

But does the fact that we do not support them at the elections imply that we are cut off from the Labour Parties, the independents, the social democrats, the Labour Party, etc.? On the contrary, we seek alliance with them as much as we can. On every occasion we summon them for common action: for the strike, the boycott, for revolt, street fights, and especially for the workers' councils, the industrial councils. We seek them everywhere. Only not in parliament, as we used to do. This, in

69

Western Europe, belongs to a past epoch. But in the workshop, in the union and in the street – that is where we find them. That is where we win them. This is the new practice, succeeding social democratic practice. It is the Communist practice.

You, Comrade, wish to bring the social democrats, the Independents, etc., into Parliament in order to show that they are deceivers. You wish to use Parliament to show that it is of no use.

You seek to slyly deceive the workers. You put the rope round their neck and let them hang. We help them to avoid the rope. We do this because here we are able to do so. You follow the tactics of the peasant races; we those of the industrial races. This is no scorn, and no mockery. I believe that with you it was the right way. Only you should not – either in this small matter, or in the great question of parliamentarism – force on us what was good in Russia but leads to destruction here.

Finally I have only one remark to make: you say, and you have often upheld it, that in Western Europe the revolution can only begin AFTER these lower classes adjacent to the proletariat have been sufficiently shaken, neutralised or won over. As I have demonstrated that they cannot be shaken, neutralised or won at the beginning of the revolution, this latter, if your statement was correct, would be impossible. This has been told to me over and over again, from your side, and also by Comrade Zinoviev. Fortunately, however, here also your observation in the most important of questions which determine the revolution, is false. And it again proves that you see all things exclusively from the East-European point of view. I will make this clear in the last chapter.

I herewith believe to have proved that your second argument for parliamentarism is for the most part an opportunistic fraud, and that in this respect parliamentarism must now be replaced by another method of fighting, one that lacks its drawbacks and possesses greater advantages.

I recognise that in this one point your tactics can have some advantages. The Labour Government can produce some good, greater clarity. And in illegal times your tactics can be profitable. We recognise that. But just as once we needed to say to the revolutionists and reformists: we prize the development of self-consciousness in the workers above everything, even above small advantages. We now say to you, Lenin and your "Right" comrades: we prize above all the ripening of the masses towards will and deed. Hereto all things have to be made subservient in Western Europe. We will see who is right, the "Left" or Lenin. I do not doubt one moment. We will defeat you, as we did Troelstra, Henderson, Renaudel and Legien.

This here is the place to discuss the mutual relationship between party, class and mass in Western Europe.

This matter is also of the greatest importance: as important as the power of banking capital, and the UNITY of all great and small bourgeois classes it engenders. The relation between party, class and mass in Western Europe differs widely from that of Russia, and like the unity of the bourgeois classes it is due to the power of banking capital.

Our tactics must be directed toward and based on a true understanding of that relationship. Whoever does not understand this relationship, cannot understand the, tactics for Western Europe.

Let us again take Germany as an example. Not only because, with England, it is industrially the most highly developed country, but also because it offers the most developed statistics.

As we have often observed already, it has a proletariat of about twenty million actual workers: about fourteen million industrial and some six million agricultural. What does this mean? That, counting children, non-workers and the aged, this proletariat comprises at least half – and probably more – of the total population of Germany.

We have seen, however, that in the revolution the proletariat stands alone, and that the opponents of the proletariat, of the revolution, by virtue of their arms and their organisation, even to this day are so powerful that they can only be conquered by means of the unity of the entire proletariat. And because of banking capital their power is such that unity alone does not suffice: that a conscious, determined unity, a truly Communist unity is needed.

Two facts therefore are certain: the proletariat is very numerous, it comprises more than half the population; and the opposition, in spite of this, is so powerful that the unity of the proletariat, real Communist unity is necessary.

Only thus can Capitalism be overthrown, and can the revolution conquer.

What follows from these two facts?

Firstly, that the dictatorship of a Party, of a Communist Party, cannot exist here in Germany, as it did in Russia, where a few thousand dominated the proletariat. Here, in order to conquer capital, the dictatorship must be exercised by the class itself, the entire class (10).

It is not, we insistently repeat, for any radical romantic, aesthetic, heroic or intellectual reason, but for the most simple and concrete fact-one moreover that is only too much felt by the German proletariat: that highly organised German monopoly banking capital is so powerful, a unites the entire bourgeoisie.

The same cause that unites the entire bourgeoisie makes it necessary that the entire class should exercise its dictatorship.

A United Proletariat Necessary.

From the above mentioned causes there follows secondly: that at the beginning and during the course of the revolution the masses are divide into two hostile camps. By masses we mean the proletariat and the other working class combined.

These latter (petty-bourgeois, peasants, intellectuals, etc.) in the beginning and during the course of the revolution are hostile to the greater part of the proletariat. Between the proletariat on the one side and the rest of the masses on the other, there is an antithesis. Class and mass in Western Europe are not one, nor can they become so at the start, and in the first stages of the revolution.

Finally from the numerical relations of the proletariat towards the other classes, and from the fact that the proletariat must be united in order to win, there follows, as I have shown above, that the relative importance of the class, as opposed to the power of leaders, must be very great; that the power of the leaders, with regard to that of the class, must be small, and likewise that in all likelihood in Germany power cannot come into the hands of some few leaders.

If we consider the character of German industry, its concentration in great numbers of centres, this goes without saying. How great, how numerous the leadership will be, cannot as yet be ascertained, it can only be stated that it will be extended over a great number of persons.

And thus, after Germany, it is in the first place in England – and, though to a lesser degree, all over Western Europe.

And this fact that the entire class must exercise its dictatorship, how does it affect the Communist Party?

From this fact follows that the task of the Communist Party in Western Europe consists almost exclusively of preparing the class and making it conscious for the revolution and the dictatorship.

In all its actions and all its tactics the Party must always bear in mind that the revolution must be made, and the dictatorship exercised not by the Party alone, but by the class.

The task can only be fulfilled if the Communist Party consists of politically truly conscious and convinced revolutionaries, who are ready for any deed, any sacrifice, and if all the half-baked and wavering elements are kept off by means of its programme, by action, and especially by the very tactics.

For only thus, only by preserving this purity, the Party will be able to make the class truly revolutionary and Communist, through its propaganda, its slogans, and by taking the lead in all actions. The Party can take the lead only by being always absolutely pure itself.

How large the Communist Party will become through this action cannot be predetermined. We desire, of course, that it may be as big as possible. But the entire tactics and the entire struggle must be dominated by this principle: better a thousand members that are good, than a hundred thousand that are bad. For these latter cannot accomplish the revolution and the dictatorship of the proletariat.

It all depends on the purity and the firmness of the Communist Party, how far its power will reach; and how much it will influence the masses. Also the quality of the leaders depends to some degree on its tactics.

In other words, Comrade Lenin, we must never follow the tactics you followed in 1902 and 1903, when you formed the Party that has made the revolution.

Menshevist Tactics would Ruin Proletariat.

All the social democrats of Russia at that time were of the opinion that a proletarian organisation ought to be created, and they agreed that this organisation was to be obtained by means of a blind imitation of German social democracy; all this has finally crystallised into the Menshevist Party. The later Menshevists dreamed of building a big Labour Party, in which the masses would be able to find the road to their action. Such a party would have to accept all those who adopted its programme, it would have to be democratically conducted, and would find its revolutionary way by means of free criticism, and free discussion. It was against this alluring image, Comrade Lenin, that you directed all the blows of your criticism, and not only because such a party was impossible under Czarism, and an illusion, but mainly because "behind this illusion, there lurked the immense danger of opportunism."

The tactics of the Menshevists would mean that the most wavering and hesitating elements would obtain a decisive influence on the party of the proletariat. This you wished to prevent, and that is why you took care that the programme (in the well known first article), and the tactics also, should always be such that this was impossible (11).

As you did then, we of the Left Wing wish to do now in the Third International. Through our very programme and tactics we wish to chase away all vacillating and opportunist elements; we only wish to accept the truly Communist, truly revolutionary ones, we wish to carry out truly communist action. And all this exclusively with a view to inspiring the entire class with communist spirit, and of preparing it for the revolution and the dictatorship.

This latter, the preparation, is of course a process – a process of interaction. Every action, every partial revolution advances the class, brings it nearer to the party, and the stronger class means greater strength for each new struggle, and also for the party. Thus party, a class come into ever closer contact, and finally they grow into one whole.

This, therefore, is our purpose: the Party, small or large, does everything in its power to further the ripening of the class for revolution and dictatorship, as this class stands alone in the revolution, without the help of the peasants.

However, there is yet another means to obtain this. Besides the political party we have as our weapon the Arbeiter-Union, based on the industrial organisation. What the party is for political action, the Union is for economic action.

And just as the numerical and class relations for Germany and Western Europe, which I have quoted, clearly demonstrate that the party cannot exercise the dictatorship, so these figures, these class relations, this unity of all bourgeois classes against the revolution, this inevitable unity of the proletariat against them, and this necessity of the entire class exercising the dictatorship, and becoming for the most part communist, demonstrate the iron necessity that no Trade Union, nor Arbeiter-Union or Industrial League, nor IWU or Shop Stewards' Movement can ever presume to exercise the dictatorship.

They, both of them, party as well as Arbeiter-Union, each in its own sphere, and with every possible mutual support, must do all they can to prepare the class. For the time being, Party and Union are separate as yet. For, like all Trade Unions, the Union also has to fight for small improvements, and is therefore constantly exposed to opportunist and reformist influences. Only a truly communist party can subordinate everything to the revolution.

From the necessity of this development in Western Europe (which has sprung up through the power of banking capital), it is also clearly evident that those who already now in the beginning and course of the revolution wish to place the Arbeiter-Union, the Industrial Union, the industrial organisation, above the Party, or who even wish to abolish the latter, are wrong.

Gradually, as the Party grows stronger, as the Union grows, as the class becomes more and more communist, as the revolution approaches its goal, class, party and Arbeiter-Union or Industrial Union closely approach one another. In the end the Party, the Union and the class are all equivalent, and are blended into one whole.

Finally, of course, the power and the unity of all

bourgeois classes, and the necessary unity of the entire proletariat, make strong centralisation and strict discipline, in the Party as well as in the Union, absolutely necessary.

It is the task of the German and English, the West-European and American proletariat to combine centralisation and discipline with the strictest control of, with power over, the leadership.

For only thus can the West-European and American proletariat conquer, through the blending of centralisation in the leadership, and the control of the membership.

It need hardly be explained here that also after the revolution the dictatorship of the entire class, and the communist spirit of the whole proletariat in Western Europe and America are absolutely necessary. For here the counterrevolution is so powerful, that if these two conditions were not fulfilled – if, for instance, a new class of rulers sprung up, out of the intellectuals and the bureaucracy – the revolution would soon perish. Now already the tactics must be on the lookout to prevent this.

How different from Russia all this is!

How different from Russia where, as a result of the economic conditions, as a result of class relations – and rightly, therefore – a handful of people rule the Party, where an infinitesimally small party rules the class, and a minutely small class the entire nation; where no Arbeiter-Union is needed, where the class, and the great majority of the remaining working masses, the small peasants, were one with the revolution!

Whoever fails to understand from the productive and class relations of Western Europe what the relations between the leaders, the party, the class and the masses are, does not understand a thing of the revolution in Western Europe, nor of its necessary stipulations. Whoever wishes to conduct the west-European revolution according to the tactics and by the road of the Russian revolution, is not qualified to lead it.

The Left Wing Tactics.

From these West-European, and to some extent also from the American and Anglo-Colonial relations, it is therefore perfectly obvious that there is only one kind of tactics that in Western Europe (and North America) can lead to victory, and these are the tactics of the Left Wing, in the name of which I speak. For these claim that the leaders shall have relatively little power in relation to the class, and the class shall have relatively far greater power. They say that for the time being the class and the rest of the masses cannot be one. They claim that the entire class shall become truly communist, through truly communist propaganda, that therefore party and class shall become one. These, in order to obtain that end, wish to destroy the bourgeois Trade Unions, and replace them by communist industrial organisations, thus making those organisations, substitutes for the Trade Unions, the greatest of class organisations (in Germany they number ten million proletarians already), equal to the class. They are against parliamentarism, thus making every worker, and consequently the entire proletariat, independently revolutionary, which is to say communist.

They, the Left party, act in perfect accordance therefore with class relations as they really are in Western Europe, and are entirely in the right against the Executive Committee, the Congress of the Third International, and you, Comrade Lenin.

Only quite recently you said to a British delegation that in England a quite small Communist Party would be able to accomplish the revolution. Here, again, you speak as a Russian, and judge things be the Russian example. And it is on such mistaken notions that the tactics of the Executive and of the International are based! (12).

Those however who think, and say, and propagate these views, do not understand class relations in Western Europe and North America (13).

78

To these observations I need only add that where I speak of the unity of party and class, that is attained at last, and of the possibility of the entire proletariat in Western Europe and America becoming communist, I mean unity as big as possible, and a large part of the proletariat. I represent total unity and the entire proletariat as the Ideal, as the goal towards which we must tend, as the aim of our tactics. In all probability it will be impossible and unnecessary to completely achieve it. But the unity of party and class, and the portion of the proletariat that has to become communist, are so immeasurably greater here than in Russia, that this ideal in the tactics must be brought to the fore (14).

Lenin's Third Argument.

Next I come to your third argument: the Russian examples. You mention them repeatedly (on pp. 6-9 they occur several times). I have read them with the greatest attention, and, as I admired them before, I do now. I have been on your side ever since 1903. Also when I did not know your motives as yet – the connections being cut off – as at the time of the Brest-Litovsk peace, I defended you with your own motives. Your tactics were certainly brilliant for Russia, and it is owing to these tactics that the Russians have triumphed. But what does this prove for Western Europe? Nothing, according to my idea, or very little. The Soviets, the dictatorship of the proletariat, the methods for the revolution and for reconstruction, all this we accept. Also your international tactics have been – so far at least – exemplary. But for your tactics for the countries of Western Europe it is different. And this is only natural.

How could the tactics in the East and West of Europe possibly be the same? Russia, a chiefly agricultural country, but with an industrial capitalism that was only partially highly developed, and very small compared to the land. And, moreover, fed to a large extent by foreign capital! In Western Europe, and especially in England and Germany, it is just the opposite. With you: still all the old-fashioned forms of capital, from usury capital upwards. With us: almost exclusively a highly developed banking capital.

With you: immense remains of feudal and pre-feudal times, and even from the time of the tribe, of barbarism. With us, and especially in England and Germany: all things, agriculture, commerce, transport, industry, under the domination of the most developed capitalism. With you: immense remains of serfdom, the poor peasants, and in the country a declining middle class. With us: even the poor peasants in connection with modern production, transport, technique and exchange. And in the city as well as in the country the middle class, including the lower layers, in direct contact with the big capitalists.

You still have classes with which the rising proletariat can unite. The very existence of these classes helps. The same applies of course to the political parties. And with us, nothing of all this.

Of course, compromising in all directions, as you so captivatingly describe it, even making use of the rifts between the Liberals and the landowners, was alright for you. With us it is impossible. Consequently the difference in tactics between the East and the West. Our tactics fit our conditions. They are just as good as yours were under Russian conditions.

I find your Russian examples especially on pages 12, 13, 26, 27, 37, 40, 51 and 52. But no matter what these examples may mean for the Russian trade union question (p 27), for Western Europe they mean nothing at all, as here the proletariat needs far stronger weapons. As far as parliamentarism is concerned, your examples have been taken from a period when the revolution had not broken out (pp. 16, 26, 41 and 51 for instance), and these, therefore, either do not apply to the point in question, or, in so far as you could use the parties of the poor peasants and petty-bourgeoisie, they are so different from conditions here (pp. 12, 37, 40, 41 and 51), as to mean nothing to us (15).

It seems to me, Comrade, that your utterly wrong judgment, the utterly mistaken conception of your book, and no less the tactics of the Executive in Moscow, are to be attributed exclusively to the fact that you do not know enough about relations over here, or rather that you fail to draw the right conclusions from what you know, that you judge things too much from the Russian point of view.

This means, however – and it should be emphasised here once again, as the fate of the West-European proletariat, the world proletariat, the world revolution depends on this – that neither you, nor the Moscow Executive are able to direct the West- European and consequently the World Revolution, as long as you adhere to these tactics.

You ask: is it possible that you, who wish to reform the world, cannot even form a fraction in parliament?

Labour Movement in False Grooves.

We answer: this book of yours is a proof in itself that whoever tries to do the latter is bound to lead the Labour movement into false grooves, into ruin.

The book deludes the workers of Western Europe by means of illusions, of the impossible; compromise with the bourgeois parties in the revolution.

It makes them believe in something that does not exist: the possibility of the bourgeois parties being divided in Western Europe, in the revolution. It makes them believe that here a compromise with the social patriots and the wavering elements in parliament can lead to any good, whereas it brings hardly anything but calamity.

Your book leads the West-European proletariat back into the morass, from which at the cost of the greatest efforts it has not yet escaped, but is beginning to escape.

It leads us back into the morass, in which men like Scheidemann, Clynes, Renaudel, Kautsky, MacDonald, Longuet, Vandervelde, Branting and Troelstra have landed us. (It must inevitably fill all these with great joy, and bourgeois parties likewise, if they understand it). This book is to the communist revolutionary proletariat what Bernstein's book has been for the pre-revolutionary proletariat. It is the first book of yours that is no good. For Western Europe, it is the worst book imaginable.

We, comrades of the Left Wing, must stand close together, must start everything from below upward, and must criticise as keenly as possible all those that in the Third International do not go the right way (16).

Thus the conclusion to be drawn from all these arguments about parliamentarism, is as follows: your three arguments for parliamentarism either mean very little, or are wrong. And, as in the Trade Union question, your tactics also on this point are disastrous for the proletariat. And with these mistaken or insignificant motives you hide the fact that you are bringing hundreds of thousands of opportunists into the Third International.

NOTES

1. Originally I considered this a minor point. The attitude of the Spartakus League, however, at the time of the Kapp putsch, and your opportunist brochure, opportunist even on this question, have convinced me that it is of great importance.

2. This great influence, this entire ideology of the West of Europe, of the United States and the British colonies, is not understood in Eastern Europe, in Turkey, the Balkans, etc. (to say nothing of Asia, etc.).

3. The example of Comrade Liebknecht is in itself a proof that our tactics are right. BEFORE the revolution, when imperialism was as yet at the summit of power, and suppressed every movement by martial law, he could exercise an enormous influence through his protests in parliament; DURING the revolution this was so no longer. As soon, therefore, as the workers have taken their lot into their own hands, we must let go of parliamentarism.

4. It is true that England has no poor peasants to support capital. But the middle class is correspondingly greater, and is united with capitalism. By means of this advance guard the English proletariat shows how it wants to fight: alone, and against all classes of England and its colonies. And exactly like Germany again: by setting an example. By founding a Communist Party that rejects parliamentarism, and that calls out to the entire class in England: let go of parliament, the symbol of capitalist power. Form your own party and your own industrial organisations. Rely on your own strength exclusively.

This had to be so in England, Comrade; it had to come in the long run. This pride and courage, born out of the greatest capitalism. Now that it comes at last, it comes in full force at once.

5. In England, more even than anywhere else, there is always a great danger of opportunism. Thus also our Comrade Sylvia Pankhurst, who from temperament, instinct and experience, not so much perhaps from deep study, but by mere chance, was such an excellent champion of Left Wing Communism, seems to have changed here views. She gives up anti-parliamentarism, and consequently the cornerstone of her fight against opportunism, for the sake of the immediate advantage of unity! By so doing she follows the road thousands of English Labour leaders have taken before her: the road towards submission to opportunism and all it leads to, and finally to the bourgeoisie. This is not to be wondered at. But that you, Comrade Lenin, should have induced her to do so, should have persuaded her, the only fearless leader of consequence in England, this is a blow for the Russian, for the world revolution.

One might ask why I defend anti-parliamentarism for England, whereas above I have recommended it only for those countries where the revolution has broken out. The answer must be that in the struggle it may often prove necessary to go one step so much to the Left. If, in a country so diseased with opportunism as England, the danger should arise of a young Communist Party falling back into the course of opportunism, through parliamentarism, it is a tactical necessity to defend anti-parliamentarism. And thus in many countries of Western Europe it may continue to be!

6. It is true that through the war an infinitely greater number of various elements has come down to the ranks of the proletariat. All elements, though as good as any element that is not proletarian, cling desperately to capitalism, and if need be will defend it by armed force, being hostile to Communism.

7. I lack the space here to point this out in detail. I have done it so at length in a brochure entitled *The Basis of Communism*.

8. We Dutchmen know this only too well. We have seen the "rifts" disappear

before our eyes, in our small, but, through our colonies, highly imperialist country. With us there are no longer democratic, Christian, or other parties. Even the Dutch can judge this better than a Russian, who, I regret to say, seems to judge Western Europe after Russia.

9. It is yet the question whether these "pure" Labour governments will come here. Maybe that here again you let yourself be misled by the Russian example – Kerensky. Later in this letter, I will point out why in this case, in the March days in Germany, this "pure" socialist government was not to be supported all the same.

10. The Russian Communist Party at the time of Yudenitch's and Denikin's attacks, numbered 13,287 men, not one ten thousandth part of the population of 150 million. Through special weeks of propaganda the number, by January 1920, increased to 220,000. Now it is no more than 600,000, 52% of which are workers.

11. The quotations are from Radek.

12. I point out here the contradiction between this opinion and the effort of winning millions of wavering elements to the Third International. This contradiction is another proof of the opportunism of your tactics.

13. A very strong proof of how the Board of the Third International judges all things from the Russian standpoint, is the following: after the German revolution had been beaten down, after the Bavarian and Hungarian revolutions had been crushed, Moscow said to the German and Hungarian proletariat:

"Be comforted, and bear up, for in March and July 1917, we were also defeated; but in November we won. As it went with us, it will go with you."

And to be sure, this time again Moscow is saying the same to the Czecho-Slovakian workers. But the Russians won in November exclusively because the poor peasants no longer supported Kerensky! Where, Executive Committee, are the millions of poor peasants in Germany, Bavaria, Hungary, and in Czecho-Slovakia? There are none. Your words are just utter nonsense. The perniciousness of these Moscow tactics, however, does not lie solely in that they console the workers by means of a false image, but more especially in the fact that they fail to draw the right conclusion from the defeat in Germany, Bavaria, Hungary and Czecho-Slovakia. The lesson they teach is this:

"Destroy your Trade Unions, and form industrial unions, thus rendering your Party and your class strong internally."

Instead of this lesson, however, we only hear: "It will go with you as it did with us!." Is it not high time that, against these Moscow tactics , there should arise, all over Western Europe, one firmly organised, iron opposition? It is a question of life and death for the world revolution itself. And also for the Russian revolution.

14. With regard to this we must bear in mind that here we are always speaking of a disarmed proletariat. If through some reason or other, through a new war, or later on, in the course of the revolution, the proletariat should once more obtain arms, the above-mentioned conditions do not count.

15. To deal with all these Russian examples would be too monotonous. I request the reader to read them all over. He will see that what I have said above is right.

16. Personally I believe that in countries where the revolution is far off as yet, and the workers are not yet strong enough to make it, parliamentarism can still be used. The sharpest criticism of the parliamentary delegates is necessary in that case. Other comrades, I believe, are of a different opinion.

Opportunism in the Third International

The question of opportunism in our own ranks is of such immense weight that I must deal with it more at length.

Comrade! With the establishment of the Third International, opportunism has not died in our ranks either. We see it in all Communist parties in all countries. Also it would be truly miraculous and against all the laws of development if that which killed the Second International did not live in the Third.

On the contrary, just as the fight between anarchism and social democracy was fought in the Second International, that between opportunism and revolutionary Marxism will be fought in the Third.

This time again Communists will go into parliament to become leaders. Trade Unions and Labour parties will be supported for the sake of votes in the elections. Instead of parties being founded for Communism, Communism will be used to found parties. But parliamentary compromises with social patriots and bourgeois elements will once more come into use, as after all the revolution in Western Europe is going to be a slow process. Freedom of speech will be suppressed, and all good Communists expelled. In a word, all the practice of the Second International will come to life again.

The Left Wing must oppose this; it has to be there, to wage this fight, as it was there in the Second International. Herein the Left Wing must be supported by all Marxists and revolutionaries, even if they are of the opinion that the Left Wing is mistaken in detail – for opportunism is our greatest enemy. Not only, as you say (p. 13) outside, but also within our ranks.

It would be a thousand times worse, that opportunism,

with its devastating effect on the soul and the strength of the proletariat, should again slip in, than that the Left Wing should be too radical. The Left Wing, even though at times it goes too far, always remains revolutionary. The Left Wing will alter its tactics as soon as they are not right. The opportunist Right will grow ever more opportunist, will sink ever further into the morass, will corrupt the workers to an ever greater extent. Not in vain have we learned from twenty-five years of struggle.

Opportunism is the plague of the Labour movement, the death of the revolution. Opportunism has brought about all evils; reformism, the war, the defeat and the death of the revolution in Hungary and Germany. Opportunism is the cause of disaster. And it exists in the Third International.

What do I need so many words for? Look around you, Comrade. Look into yourself, and into the Executive Committee! Look into all countries of Europe.

Feeble Criticism.

Read the papers of the British Socialist Party, now the Communist Party. Read ten, twenty numbers of this paper; read the feeble criticism against the Trade Unions, the Labour Party, the Members of Parliament, and compare this to the paper of the Left Wing. A comparison between these two will show you that opportunism is approaching the Third International, in immense masses. Once more (through support of the counter-revolutionary workers) to obtain power in Parliament. A power after the pattern of the Second International. Remember too that soon the USP will enter the Third International, and numerous other Centre parties besides! Do you not believe that if you compel these parties to expel Kautsky that a swarm of tens of thousands of other opportunists will come? The entire measure of this expulsion is childish. An innumerable stream of opportunists is approaching (1) – especially since your brochure.

Look at the Dutch Communist Party, once called the

Bolshevists of Europe. And rightly so, taking into account the conditions. Read the brochure about the Dutch Party, how utterly already it has been corrupted by the opportunism of the Second International. During the war, and after it, and even to this day, it has pledged itself to the Entente. This once brilliant party has become an example of equivocality and deceit.

But look at Germany, Comrade, the land where the revolution has started. There opportunism lives and thrives. We were utterly amazed to hear that you defended the attitude of the KPD during the March days. But fortunately we learned from your brochure that you did not know the actual course of development. You sanctioned the attitude of the KPD-Zentrale, that offered loyal opposition to Ebert, Scheidemann, Hilferding and Crispien, but you evidently did not know, at the time of writing the brochure, that this happened at the same moment Ebert organised troops against the German proletariat, whose general strike was still spread all over Germany, and in which the great majority of the Communist mass strove to bring the revolution, if not to victory (perhaps this was hardly possible as yet), at any rate to a higher strength Whilst the mass by means of strikes and armed revolt, conducted the revolution into a further stage (there has never been anything more hopeful or gigantic than the revolt in the Ruhr region, and the general strike), the leaders offered parliamentary compromises. In so doing they supported Ebert against the revolution in the Ruhr region (2). If ever an example proved how damnable the use of parliamentarism is in the revolution, this is it. You see, Comrade, that is parliamentary opportunism, that is compromise with the social patriots and the Independents, which we refuse to accept, and which you try to further.

And, Comrade, what has already become of the industrial councils in Germany? You and the Executive of the Third International had advised the Communists to unite with all the other trends, in order to obtain the leadership of the Trade Unions. And what has happened? The opposite. The industrial Zentrale has well-nigh developed into an instrument of the

Trade Unions. The Trade Unions are an octopus, strangling everything living that comes within its reach.

Comrade, if you read and investigate everything that is being done in Germany, in Western Europe, I have full confidence that you will come over to our side. Just as I believe that your experiences in the Third International will convert you to our tactics.

However, if opportunism proceeds thus in Germany, how will it be in France and England!

You see, Comrade, these are the leaders we do not want. That is the unity of mass and leader that we do not want. And that is the iron discipline, the military obedience, submission and servility that we do not want.

Permit us to add here one word to the Executive Committee, and especially to Radek: the Executive Committee has had the insolence to demand of the KAPD that they should expel Wolffheim and Laufenberg, instead of leaving them to settle this for themselves. It has threatened the KAPD, and has pandered to the central parties, such as the USP. But it did not demand of the Italian Party that it should expel the Zentrale which, through its offer, was partly responsible for the murder of Communists in the Ruhr region. It did not demand of the Dutch Party that it should expel Wijnkoop and Van Ravesteyn, who during the war, offered Dutch ships to the Entente. This does not mean to say that I myself wish those comrades to be expelled. On the contrary, I hold them to be good comrades, who have gone wrong only because the development, the beginning of the West- European revolution, is so terribly difficult. We, all of us over here, still make many big mistakes. Moreover, expulsion at present, from this International, would be of no avail.

I only point this out to demonstrate by another example how fiercely opportunism is raging already in our own ranks. For the Moscow Central Committee has committed this injustice against the KAPD only, because for its opportunist world tactics it did not want the really revolutionary elements, but the opportunist Independents, etc.. It has deliberately used the tactics of Wolffheim and Laufenberg against the KAPD for the most miserably opportunist of reasons, although it knew that the KAPD did NOT agree with those tactics. Because it wants to have masses around it, like the Trade Unions and the political parties, no matter whether those masses are communist or not.

Two other actions of the Third International prove clearly where it is drifting. The first is the expulsion of the Amsterdam Bureau, the ONLY group of revolutionary Marxists and theoreticians in Western Europe, that has never wavered. The second section, which is almost more serious, is the treatment of the KAPD, the ONLY party in Western Europe which, as an organisation, as a whole, from its very origin onwards, has conducted the revolution as it should be conducted. Whilst the Centre parties, the Independents, the French and English Centre, who always betrayed the revolution, were allured by all possible means, the KAPD, the real revolutionaries, were treated as enemies. These are bad signs, Comrade.

In a word: the Second International is still alive, or alive again, in our midst. And opportunism leads to ruin. And because this is so, and because opportunism is very strong amongst us, far stronger than I could ever have imagined, the Left Wing has to be there. Even if there should be no other good reasons for its existence, it would have to be there as an opposition, to counterbalance opportunism.

Alas, Comrade, if only you had followed the tactics of the Left Wing in the Third International; those tactics, that are nothing but the "pure" tactics of the Bolshevists in Russia, adapted to West-European (and North American) conditions!

If only, as stipulations and statutes for the Third International, you had proposed and carried through economic organisation in industrial organisations and workers' unions (into which, if need be, industrial unions on a shop floor basis might have been introduced), and political organisation in parties which reject parliamentarism!

Then you would in the first place have had, in all countries, absolutely firm kernels, parties that could really carry out the revolution, parties that would gradually have gathered the masses around them, through their own example, in their own country, and not through pressure from outside. Then you would have had economic organisations that would have annihilated the counter-revolutionary Trade Unions (syndicalist as well as free). And then with ONE stroke you would have cut off the way for all opportunists. For these can thrive only where there is plotting with the counter-revolution.

Then, likewise – and this is by far the most important point – you would have educated the workers into independent fighters to a very high degree, as far as it is possible in the present stage.

If you, Lenin, and you, Bukharin and Radek, had done this, had chosen these tactics, with your authority and experience, your strength and genius, and if you had helped us to eradicate the faults that cling to us as yet, and to our tactics, then we would have achieved a Third International that was perfectly firm internally, and unshakable externally, an International which would gradually have gathered the entire proletariat around it, through the force of its example, and which would have built Communism.

It is true that there are no tactics without defeat. But these would have suffered least defeat, and would most easily have recovered from it; they would have gone the quickest way, and would have won the quickest and surest victory. Yours lead to repeated defeat for the proletariat.

However, you have rejected this because, instead of conscious, steadfast fighters, you wanted partly or totally unconscious masses.

NOTES

1. In Halle, in one day alone, 500,000 new members came under leaders which only a short while before they themselves had recognised to be worse than the Scheidemann lot. And in Tours, three quarters of the French Socialist Party joined, which until quite recently were for the most part social patriots.

2. Comrade Pannekoek, who thoroughly knows Germany, had predicted this. If the leaders of the Spartakus League were placed before the choice between Parliament and Revolution, they would choose Parliament.

Conclusions

Finally I have to make a few observations regarding your last chapter: "Conclusions," perhaps the most important of your entire book. Again I was delighted with it, as long as I thought of the Russian revolution. But over and over again the thought came into my head: the tactics that are brilliant for Russia are bad here. They lead to defeat here.

You assert here, comrade (pp. 68-74), that in a certain stage of development the masses must be attracted, millions and millions of them. The propaganda for "pure" Communism, that collected the avant-garde, and educated it, suffices no longer in that stage. Now is the time, and next follow once again your opportunist methods that I have already refuted: taking advantage of "rifts," of petty-bourgeois elements, etc.

Comrade, this chapter is also completely wrong.

You judge as a Russian, not as an international Communist who knows real West-European capitalism.

Almost every word of this chapter, wonderful though it may be for the knowledge of your revolution, is wrong for big industrial capitalism, for the trusts and monopoly capitalism.

I will demonstrate this here: first in small matters.

Still Need for Propaganda.

You write about Communism in Western Europe.

"The vanguard of the West-European proletariat has been won" (p. 70). This is wrong, Comrade. "The period of propaganda is past" (p. 69). This is not true. "The proletarian vanguard has been won over ideologically." This is not so, Comrade. This stands in line (and it proceeds from the same mentality) with what I read in Bukharin, not long ago: "English capitalism is bankrupt." I also read in Radek similar fantasies, that were closer to astrology than astronomy. Nothing of this is true. Except for Germany, there is no vanguard anywhere yet. Neither in England, nor France, nor Belgium, nor Holland, nor, if I am well informed, in most of the Scandinavian countries. There are only a few "Eclaireurs," who do not agree yet about the course that must be followed (1). "The period of propaganda is past" is a terrible lie.

No, Comrade, this period is just beginning in Western Europe. There is no firm kernel anywhere as yet.

What we need here is such a kernel, hard as steel, clear as glass. And this is where we should begin herewith to build up a big organisation. In this respect we are here in the stage you were in 1903, or even before, in the Iskra period. Comrade, conditions here are far riper than we are, but that is no reason why we should let ourselves be carried away, to begin without a kernel!

For the time being we of Western Europe, the Communist parties in England, France, Belgium, Holland, Scandinavia, Italy, even the KAPD in Germany, must remain small, not because we want to, but because otherwise we cannot become strong.

An example: Belgium. Except for Hungary, before the revolution, there is no country where the proletariat is as corrupted by reformism as Belgium. If at this moment Communism should become a mass movement there (with parliamentarism, etc.), the vultures, the profiteers etc. of opportunism would swoop down on it immediately and drag it to destruction. And it is the same everywhere.

For that reason, because the Labour movement here is very weak as yet, and almost completely trapped in opportunism, because so far Communism is hardly anything, and must fight (on the questions of parliamentarism and the

Trade Unions and on all others) until we attain the highest lucidity and clarity, until everything has been made theoretically as clear as possible.

A sect, therefore, says the Executive Committee. Certainly a sect, if that is what you want to call the kernel of a movement that conquers the world.

Comrade, there was a time when your movement, the Bolsheviks, was also small and insignificant. It was because it was small, and voluntarily remained so for a long time that it kept itself pure. And through this, and this exclusively it became powerful. We also want to proceed in this way.

This is a question of the utmost importance. Not only the West-European, but also the Russian revolution depends on this. Beware, Comrade! You know that Napoleon in trying to spread modern capitalism all over Europe was finally wrecked and had to make way for reaction, when he had arrived; where there was not only too much of the middle ages, but especially too little capitalism.

These, your minor assertions, are not true. I will now proceed to the bigger ones, to the most important of all you say: that now the time has come without propaganda to win the millions for "pure" Communism, through the opportunist policy you describe. Comrade, even if you were right in the small matters, if the Communist Parties here were actually strong enough, this would be utterly wrong from beginning to end. Pure propaganda for the new Communism, as I have often said already, will be necessary here in Western Europe, from the beginning of the revolution to the very end. Because (this point is of such importance that it has to be constantly repeated) it is the workers, the workers alone, who must bring Communism. Of the other classes they have nothing to expect, in any considerable measure, until the revolution is finished.

You say (p. 72) : that period of the revolution has started in which we have the vanguard, and in which:

1. all class powers that are against us have become sufficiently disarranged, have fought sufficiently amongst themselves, have been sufficiently weakened by the struggle that surpasses their strength;

2. all vacillating, undecided elements, the petty- bourgeoisie, petty-bourgeois democracy, have been sufficiently unmasked before the people, have exposed themselves sufficiently through their bankruptcy.

Well, Comrade, this is Russian. In the Russian government body, which was rotten through and through, these were the conditions for the revolution.

In the modern, really big-capitalist states, however, the conditions will be altogether different. The big bourgeois parties will stand together in opposition to Communism, will not get disarranged, and the petty-bourgeoisie will stand by them. Not in an absolute sense, of course, but to such an extent that it has to determine our tactics.

Character of Western European Revolution.

In Western Europe we must expect a revolution that is a tenacious struggle on either side, with a firm organisation on the part of the bourgeoisie and the petty-bourgeoisie. The immense organisations of capitalism and of the workers prove this.

These, therefore, we have to organise likewise with the very best weapons, the best form of organisation, the best and strongest methods of fighting (not with weak ones).

It is here, and not in Russia, that the real struggle between capital and labour will be fought. Because here there is real capital.

Comrade, if you think that (from a tendency for theoretical purity), I exaggerate, just look at Germany. There you have an utterly bankrupt, almost desperate State. But all classes, big and petty bourgeois alike, as well as the peasant classes, stand firmly united against Communism. Thus it will be everywhere with us.

It is true that just at the end of the development of the revolution, when the most terrible crisis breaks out, when we are quite close to victory, the unity of the bourgeois classes will perhaps disappear, and some of the petty bourgeois and peasants will come to us. But what good is that to us? We must determine our tactics for the beginning and the course of the revolution.

Because this is so, and has to be so (because of the class relations and even more the relations of production) , the proletariat stands alone.

Because it stands alone, it can only triumph if it gains greatly in spiritual strength.

And as this is the only way it can triumph, propaganda for "pure" Communism is needed here until the very end (quite the contrary to Russia).

Without this propaganda, the West-European, and consequently the Russian proletariat, is lost.

And the same holds true of the Executive in Moscow.

Whilst I was writing these last few pages, the news came through that the International had adopted your tactics and those of the Executive. The West-European delegates have let themselves be dazzled by the brilliance of the Russian revolution. All right, we will take up the fight in the Third International.

We, Comrade, your old friends Pannekoek, Roland Holst, Rutgers and myself, truer than which you cannot find, on hearing of your West-European tactics, asked ourselves what could have caused them. Opinions differed greatly. The one said: the economic condition of Russia is so bad that, after all, it needs peace. For that reason, Comrade Lenin wants to gather around him as much power as possible: the Independents, Labour Party, etc., so that they may help him to obtain peace.

The other said: he wishes to hasten the general European revolution. Therefore millions have to join. That is the reason for his opportunism.

I myself believe, as I have said before, that you misunderstand European conditions, the state of things.

However this may be, Comrade, and from what motives you may act, if you go on with these tactics, you will suffer the most terrible defeat, and you will lead the proletariat into the most terrible defeat.

For if you wish to save Russia, the Russian revolution, by means of these tactics, you collect non-Communist elements. You join them to us, the real Communists, whilst we do not as yet have a firm kernel! With this medley of dead Trade Unions, with a mass of half or quarter Communists, in which there is no solid kernel, you want to fight against the best organised capital in the world, with all the non-proletarian classes on its side. It goes without saying that in the battle this medley will fall apart, and the great mass will take flight.

Why German Workers must not be Defeated.

Comrade, a crushing defeat, of the German proletariat for instance, is the signal for a general attack on Russia.

If you wish to make the revolution here, with this hodgepodge of Labour Party and Independents, French Centre and the Italian Party, etc., and with these Trade Unions, the outcome cannot be otherwise. The governments will not even fear such a load of opportunists.

If however you form internally firm, radical groups, firm (though small) parties, then the government will fear these parties, as only these carry away the masses in great deeds in the revolution – as the Spartakus League has proved in the beginning – then the governments will have to release Russia, and finally, when the parties will thus, through these "pure" tactics, have grown powerful, victory will be ours. These our

"Left" tactics, therefore, are the best; nay the only ones that bring salvation for us and for Russia alike.

Your tactics on the other hand are Russian. They were excellent in a country where an army of millions of poor peasants stood ready, and where there was a wavering, desperate middle class. Here they are no good.

I must finally refute your assertion and that of many of your associates, upon which I have already touched in the third chapter; that the revolution in Western Europe can only begin after the lower, democratic layers of capitalism have been sufficiently shaken, neutralised or won.

This assertion also, in one of the most weighty questions of the revolution, proves once more that you consider everything from a purely East- European point of view. And this assertion is wrong.

For the proletariat in Germany and England is so numerous, so powerful through its organisation, that it can make the revolution, its beginning and development without, and in opposition to all these classes. And even that it must make the revolution, driven by sufferings in Germany.

And it can only do so, if it follows the right tactics, if it founds its organisation on a shop floor basis, and rejects parliamentarism; if only it strengthens the workers in this way!

We of the Left Wing, therefore, choose our tactics not only for the reason mentioned above, but especially also because the West-European proletariat, and in the first place the German and English proletariat, by itself alone, if only it grows conscious and united, is so immensely strong, that it can win in this simple manner. The Russian proletariat had to take roundabout ways, being too weak by itself, and it has done so brilliantly, in a manner far surpassing all that the world proletariat has ever achieved. But the West-European proletariat can triumph by the straight, clear road.

Thus also this assertion of yours has been refuted.

There remains one argument still to be refuted, one which I have read over and over again with the "Right" Communists, which I heard from the Russian Trade Union leader, Losovski, and which is to be found also with you: "The crisis will drive the masses to Communism, even if we retain the bad Trade Unions and parliamentarism." This is a very weak argument. For we have no idea how big the crisis is going to be. Will it be as deep in England and France as it is now in Germany? Secondly, this argument (the "mechanical argument of the Third International"), has proved how weak it is during the last six years. In Germany the misery during the last years of the war was terrible. The revolution did not break out. It was terrible in 1918 and 1919. The revolution did not triumph. The crisis in Hungary, Austria, the Balkans and Poland is terrible. The revolution did not come, or did not win, not even when the Russian armies were quite near. But in the third place the argument turns against yourself, for if the crisis should bring about the revolution in any case, the better "Left" tactics might be just as well adopted.

The examples of Germany, Hungary, Bavaria, Austria, Poland and the Balkans however, all prove that crisis and misery do not suffice. They have the most terrible economic crisis, and yet the revolution does not break out. There must be another cause yet, which brings the revolution about, and which, if it does not work, causes the delay, or the collapse of the revolution. This cause is the spirit of the masses. And it is your tactics, Comrade, which fail to sufficiently awaken the spirit of the masses in Western Europe, which does not sufficiently strengthen it, which leaves it as it was. In the course of writing I have pointed out that banking capital, the trusts, the monopolies and the West-European and North American state formed by them, and dependent on them, as they are, unite all bourgeois classes, big as well as small, into one whole against the revolution.

But this force, uniting society and the state against the revolution, goes even further. Banking capital itself organised the working class in a previous period, in the period of evolution, against the revolution: educating, uniting and organising them. And in what way? In the Trade Unions (Syndicalist as well as free), and in the social-democratic parties. By forcing them to fight only for reforms, capital turned these Trade Unions and Labour parties into counter-revolutionary forces for the maintenance of the State and society. Because of big capital, Trade Unions and Labour parties became props of capitalism. As, however, these organisations consist of workers, and of almost the majority of workers, and as the revolution cannot be made without the workers, these organisations must be destroyed before the revolution can succeed. And how are they to be destroyed? By changing their spirit. And their spirit can only be changed by making the spirit of the members independent to the utmost degree. And this can be done only by replacing the Trade unions with industrial unions and workers' unions, and by abolishing parliamentarism in the Labour parties. And your tactics prevent this.

It is true that German, French and Italian capitalism is bankrupt. Or rather: these capitalist States are bankrupt. The capitalists themselves, their economic and political organisations, maintain themselves and their profits, dividends and new capital are still huge. Only, however, by an extension of the circulation of paper by the State. If the German, French and Italian States fall, the capitalists fall likewise.

Crisis is Nearing.

The crisis approaches with an iron necessity. If prices rise, strike waves rise as well; if they fall, the army of the unemployed increases. Misery is spreading all over Europe, and hunger is approaching. Moreover, the world is full of new fuel. The conflict, the new revolution, is drawing near. But how will it end? Capitalism is still powerful. Germany, Italy, France and Eastern Europe are not the whole world. And in Western Europe, North America and the British Dominions, for some time to come, capitalism will hold together all classes against the proletariat. The issue therefore to a very great extent depends on our tactics and on our organisation. And your tactics are wrong.

Here in Western Europe there is only one kind of tactics: those of the Left Wing, that tells the proletariat the truth, and does not blind it with illusions. Those that, even though it may take a long time, forge the only effective weapons – the industrial organisations (uniting these into one whole), and the originally small, but pure and firm kernels, the Communist parties. Those tactics, moreover, that spread these organisations over the entire proletariat.

This has to be like this, not because we of the Left Wing want it, but because the relations of production, class relations, demand it.

At the conclusion of my exposition, I will draw them up in a concise survey, so that the worker may see everything clearly for himself.

In the first place, I imagine, there follows from it a clear image of the causes of our tactics (a clear survey of the motives of our tactics) , and the tactics themselves: banking capital dominates the whole world. Ideologically and materially it keeps the gigantic proletariat in the deepest slavery, and unites all bourgeois classes. Consequently the gigantic masses must rise and proceed to act for themselves. This is only possible through industrial organisations and the abolition of parliamentarism in the revolution.

Secondly, I will summarise the tactics of the Left Wing, and those of the Third International in a few phrases, so that the difference between your tactics and those of the Left Wing become clearly and absolutely obvious, and so that if your tactics lead to the greatest debacle, as they probably will, the workers will not lose courage, but might see there are other tactics.

The Third International believes that the West-European revolution will proceed together according to the laws and tactics of the Russian revolution.

The Left Wing believes that the West-European revolution will make and follow its own laws.

The Third International believes that the West-European revolution will be able to make compromises and alliances with petty-bourgeois and small peasant, and even with big bourgeois parties.

The Left Wing believes this is impossible.

The Third International believes that in Western Europe during the revolution there will be "rifts" and scissions between the bourgeois, petty-bourgeois and small peasant parties.

The Left Wing believes that the bourgeois and petty-bourgeois parties will form one united front until the end of the revolution.

The Third International underestimates the power of West-European and North American capital.

The Left Wing makes its tactics conform to this great power.

The Third International does not recognise the power of banking capital, the big capital which unites all bourgeois classes.

The Left Wing on the contrary bases its tactics on this unifying power.

As the Third International does not believe in the fact that in Western Europe the proletariat will stand alone, it neglects the mental development of this proletariat; which in every respect is still deeply entangled in bourgeois ideology; and chooses tactics which leave slavery and subjection to bourgeois ideas unmolested and intact.

Left-Winger to Free Workers' Minds.

The Left Wing chooses its tactics in such a way that in the first place the mind of the workers is liberated.

As the Third International does not found its tactics on freeing the mind, nor on the unity of all bourgeois and petty-bourgeois parties, but on compromises and "rifts"; it leaves the old Trade Unions intact, trying to unite them with the Third International.

As the Left Wing strives above all for freeing the mind, and believes in the unity of the bourgeois parties, it realises that the Trade Unions must be destroyed, and that the proletariat needs better weapons.

The same motives induce the Third International to support parliamentarism.

The same motives also induce the Left Wing to abolish parliamentarism.

The Third International leaves the condition of slavery such as it was in the Second.

The Left Wing wishes to change it from below upward; it seizes the evil at the root.

As the Third International does not believe that in the first place the liberation of minds is needed in Western Europe, nor that all bourgeois parties will be one in the revolution, it collects masses around it, without inquiring whether they are really Communist, without determining its tactics, on the supposition that they are – as long as it gets the masses.

The Left Wing wishes in all countries to form parties consisting exclusively of Communists, and determines its tactics accordingly. Through the example of these originally small parties, the majority of the proletariat, and therefore the masses, will be brought to Communism.

To the Third International, then, the masses in Western

Europe are a means.

To the Left Wing they are the aim.

Through these tactics (which were quite right in Russia), the Third International employs leader-politics.

The Left Wing, on the other hand, employs mass politics.

Through these tactics the Third International is leading not only the West-European, but also the Russian revolution, into ruin.

The Left Wing on the other hand, through its tactics, leads the world proletariat towards victory.

And, finally, I will gather my statements into a few theses, so that the workers who must strive for themselves to gain a clear insight into those tactics, may have them before their eyes in a concise, surveyable form. They have to be read, of course, in the light of the above exposition.

1. The tactics of the West-European revolution must be different from those of the Russian revolution.

2. For here the proletariat stands alone.

3. Here the proletariat must make the revolution all by itself, against all other classes.

4. The importance of the proletarian masses, therefore, is relatively greater, and that of the leaders smaller than in Russia.

5. Consequently, here the proletariat must have the very best weapons for the revolution.

6. The Trade Unions being insufficient weapons, they must be replaced or changed into industrial organisations, that are united into one league.

7. As the proletariat must make the revolution all alone, without help, it has to rise very high morally as well as spiritually. It is better therefore not to use parliamentarism in the revolution.

Marx had learnt from the Paris Commune the proletariat cannot use or take over the bourgeois

State for the revolution. Thus the "Left Wing" has learnt from the Russian, German, Hungarian, from the World Revolution, that the proletariat cannot use the old Socialist parties, nor the old Trade Unions for the revolution.

With fraternal greetings,
H. GORTER.

Notes

1. The English Communists for instance, with regard to the most important matter of affiliation to the Labour Party.

www.ingramcontent.com/pod-product-compliance
Lightning Source LLC
Chambersburg PA
CBHW031229280526
45784CB00004B/1505